"Every teen with obsessive-compulsive disorder (OCD) should read this book! It's going to be a must-read from now on in my OCD therapy practice. Jon Hershfield has mastered the tone, humor, and relatable nature that a book for teens must have in order to not be chucked back at their parent's head! Every parent should thank him!"

—**Natasha Daniels, LCSW**, child therapist specializing in anxiety and OCD, creator of www.atparentingsurvival.com, and author of *Anxiety Sucks*

"Jon Hershfield's *The OCD Workbook for Teens* is a must-read for teens experiencing OCD. He masterfully intertwines clinical expertise and personal voice in a way that speaks directly to the reader. This cleverly illustrated book provides the tools for teens to embark on their own personal quest to fight OCD. Importantly, it is also a useful resource for parents and clinicians seeking a better understanding of OCD and the teenage experience."

—**Maria G Fraire, PhD**, program director of the Child and Adolescent OCD Institute at McLean Hospital, and instructor in the department of psychology at Harvard Medical School

"To quote the opening of this book: 'Dude. Seriously.' This workbook not only covers the basics of OCD and its first-line treatment, exposure and response prevention (ERP), but also contains material to foster self-compassion, mindfulness, and the tolerance of uncertainty. It is written in friendly language to engage teens, and includes experiential exercises to foster engagement. I am confident that this will be a staple on the shelves of both teens with OCD and the clinicians who work with them."

—**Amy Mariaskin, PhD**, clinical psychologist, director of the Nashville OCD & Anxiety Treatment Center, and adjunct professor at Vanderbilt University

"There are so few books that *really* speak to teens where they are, in an empowering way, with solid strategies that they can apply immediately. Jon Hershfield's *The OCD Workbook for Teens* hits all the right notes—it is clever, and funny, with killer illustrations by graphic artist Sean Shinnock—and best of all, it contains practical, evidence-based tools presented in a collaborative, empathic way for teens. If you are a practitioner who works with teens, it's gonna be hard to keep this book from flying off the shelves!"

—**Lisa Coyne, PhD**, founder and director of the New England Center for OCD and Anxiety, assistant professor at Harvard Medical School, and coauthor of *Stuff That's Loud*

"Jon Hershfield successfully channels his 'inner teen' to communicate sometimes complicated aspects of treatment in relatable, effective, and cool ways. His innovative approach, along with Sean Shinnock's incredible illustrations, create a one-of-a-kind resource that will become a must-have for parents and kids alike. OCD can be complicated; defeating it shouldn't be. Hershfield has created a significant weapon against OCD, one I wish I'd had in my armory growing up."

—**Ethan S. Smith**, filmmaker, and national advocate for the International OCD Foundation

"Quieting OCD thoughts and rituals is hard work. Kids need help. As a parent, I'm ecstatic Jon's written this path to understanding and success. I'm thrilled Sean's illustrations show kids as defiant and victorious. This book is a relatable way for teens to understand their brains, get thoughts out into the open, and tackle ERP. It's a workbook that actually lets kids work out their anxiety. Take that, OCD."

—**Chris Baier**, parent of a teen with OCD; producer of *UNSTUCK*; and creator of OCDeconstruct, the first virtual OCD Conference

"Having interviewed Jon many times, I have come to appreciate his unique style of working with OCD. Throughout this book he gives the reader activities to help them embed the information he has accrued over many years. This coupled with Sean's illustrations bring the chapters to life by animating the experience that many young people go through. Two passionate people in the OCD community have produced this book."

—**Stuart Ralph**, founder of *The OCD Stories* podcast

"Practical and positive, *The OCD Workbook for Teens* brings CBT and mindfulness skills to teens in an easy-to-read and relatable way. The concepts of exposure and mindfulness can be hard to convey, yet Hershfield presents them succinctly and effectively. Sharing his own experience with OCD with humility, Hershfield brings a much-needed message of hope and optimism to teens with OCD."

—**Aureen Wagner, PhD**, director of The Anxiety Wellness Center in Cary, NC; and author of *What to Do When Your Child has Obsessive-Compulsive Disorder*

the ocd workbook for teens

mindfulness & cbt skills to help you overcome unwanted thoughts & compulsions

JON HERSHFIELD, MFT

ILLUSTRATIONS BY SEAN SHINNOCK

Instant Help Books

An Imprint of New Harbinger Publications, Inc.

INSTANT HELP, the Clock Logo, and NEW HARBINGER are trademarks of New Harbinger Publications, Inc.

Distributed in Canada by Raincoast Books

Copyright © 2021 by Jonathan Hershfield
        Instant Help Books
        An imprint of New Harbinger Publications, Inc.
        5674 Shattuck Avenue
        Oakland, CA 94609
        www.newharbinger.com

Cover design by Amy Shoup

Acquired by Jess O'Brien

Edited by Karen Schader

All Rights Reserved

Library of Congress Cataloging-in-Publication Data

Names: Hershfield, Jon, author. | Shinnock, Sean, illustrator.
Title: The OCD workbook for teens : mindfulness and CBT skills to help you overcome unwanted thoughts and compulsions / Jon Hershfield ; illustrated by Sean Shinnock.
Description: Oakland, CA : New Harbinger Publications, [2021]
Identifiers: LCCN 2020035553 (print) | LCCN 2020035554 (ebook) | ISBN 9781684036363 (trade paperback) | ISBN 9781684036370 (pdf) | ISBN 9781684036387 (epub)
Subjects: LCSH: Obsessive-compulsive disorder in adolescence--Treatment. | Cognitive therapy for teenagers.
Classification: LCC RJ506.O25 H47 2021 (print) | LCC RJ506.O25 (ebook) | DDC 618.92/891425--dc23
LC record available at https://lccn.loc.gov/2020035553
LC ebook record available at https://lccn.loc.gov/2020035554

Printed in the United States of America

24   23   22

10   9   8   7   6   5   4   3

Contents

a letter to teens

Dear Reader,

Dude.

Seriously. I really could've used this book when I was a teenager. I served my time in adolescence from 1990–1997. Horror movies were still pretty good, electronic music was just starting to get really interesting, and the technology was, well, let's just say if I died in a video game, I usually had to start the whole level over.

I have a memory of lying in the grass at my parents' home, looking up at the sky and thinking, *This is way too hard. No way should it be this hard.* I was fourteen. I can't even recall what it was that made me so unhappy, aside from always picturing things I looked at dying terrible deaths or bursting into flames, flipping out when my mother told me I had to make a cassette copy of my brother's new CD instead of buying my own CD with the exact same music on it, and the fact that I seemed absolutely incapable of *letting anything go.* If I said the wrong thing, embarrassed myself in any way, this event would just play on a loop for days on end. But not just a regular loop, the kind that picks up speed with each revolution. Acting helped, so I did all the school plays. Calling everything obsessive-compulsive disorder (OCD) helped, a little. But the truth is, I didn't really understand how to operate the machinery in my head until I was almost thirty. Then I became a therapist. Now, as an ancient man in his forties, I have the opportunity to show you some things that may help you understand what OCD is, how to develop mastery over it, and maybe even enjoy being young while you still have the time.

So, if you're reading this, you're probably having some difficulty with unwanted thoughts (obsessions) and behaviors (compulsions) that are sucking up a lot of time, energy, and joy. Maybe you looked for help and came across this book or maybe someone who cares about you got you this book. Here's what's in it. The book is made up of several "activities," which are basically short chapters that explain something you may not already know about OCD and ask you to try things that may help.

Some include materials you can download at the website for this book: http://www
.newharbinger.com/46363.

The first several chapters of the book are mostly about learning the ins and outs of the
disorder. Then I'll go on and on about this thing called mindfulness, a way of looking
at thoughts, feelings, and sensations that would have never occurred to me when I was
your age. After that, I'll share some tips and tools for using something called exposure
and response prevention (ERP) to outwit, outsmart, and outmaneuver your OCD. I'll
end with some ways to speak up and speak out about what you're going through.

Each activity will end with a sweet illustration by my man Sean Shinnock. I met this
guy at an International OCD Foundation conference, and we hit it off because we both
have a thing for monsters and twisted humor. Sean became an OCD advocate after
emerging victorious from his own battle with the disorder. Together we collaborated
on visuals that drive the main message of each activity home. I'd say, "What if we had
our hero battling a monster like this or that?" and then he'd draw something really
sick (in a good way). I've included a little "story update" caption to go with each image
so you can easily understand the main takeaway. Okay, so here we go. If you made
it this far through the workbook, you're already in the lead—with the OCD trailing
behind.

who's super jazzed about having a mental health issue?

1

for you to know

In this book, I'm going to attempt to explain to you what OCD is and what things you can do to help yourself. But first, let's address the giant workbook in the room. Being a teen comes with all kinds of changes and challenges. Your body and your brain are going through massive transformations. Your academic, social, and even family life are also going through major changes. You may be new to your diagnosis, or have had a diagnosis since you were little, or have yet to be diagnosed. But what does it actually *mean* to be diagnosed?

Everybody's got their issues. The people you see who look like they have it all together? They are often the people who are the best at hiding their problems. Their problems are often the worst. That's how they got so good at hiding them. Some issues, or traits, are easier to hide than others. I've gotten much better over the years at learning to present myself as relaxed when I'm really freaking out inside. So believe me, having issues that are visible or invisible doesn't make you any better or worse than anyone else. We all have issues. Some more common issues, the ones that sometimes make it hard to get things done, hard to relax, or hard to function at all, are given names like "symptoms." They can be physical (something going on in the body), behavioral (things you do), and/or mental (how you experience things). Headaches, rashes, difficulty sleeping, intense mood swings, difficulty concentrating—these are all examples of symptoms. When a group of symptoms occur together, are examined, and are given a name, this process of getting to the name is called a diagnosis.

Once you have a name for a group of symptoms, they can be studied by psychiatrists, psychologists, and other experts. These studies can help answer questions like: what people with these symptom clusters have in common, how long they tend to have these symptoms, who is more likely to have these symptoms, and most importantly, what kind of treatments reduce these symptoms the most effectively.

for you to do

You have this book because you've noticed symptoms in your life that might be best understood as OCD. We'll get to what that really means in the next activity, but for now, let's put some things into context.

How many people do you know who have a diagnosis of something? Could be a medical or mental health issue, like high blood pressure or depression. Write down the names of some of them.

_____   _____

_____   _____

_____   _____

_____   _____

_____   _____

_____   _____

_____   _____

For the people you named, how do you feel about them having a diagnosis?

_____

_____

_____

Does it affect your opinion of them in any way? Circle: **Yes**   **No**

What are the first words that come to mind about those people's diagnoses?

_____   _____

_____   _____

_____   _____

_____   _____

_____   _____

_____   _____

_____   _____

What are the first words that come to mind when you consider having a diagnosis yourself?

_____   _____

_____   _____

_____   _____

_____   _____

Is there any difference between how you think of others and how you think of yourself? Circle: **Yes**   **No**

If so, why do you think that is?

_____

_____

_____

more to do

While it can be really empowering to know what your diagnosis is, because then you can learn the tools to address it, let's be honest—it's also kind of a drag. At the very least, it's inconvenient. Teens have a lot of demands placed on them at once, like trying to figure out what work you want to do for the rest of your life even though you're still a kid, or learning to drive, or getting along with your parents, who seem to suddenly expect more from you, or passing whatever trigonometry is. Does right now in your life seem like an unfair time to have to address a mental health diagnosis?

Circle: **Yes**   **No**

If you circled "Yes," write about why a diagnosis feels unfair.

_____

_____

_____

_____

Now consider the reasons why now may be the *perfect* time for you to learn about and start developing mastery over your OCD. For example, you could learn tools that can help through the rest of your life. Write down your reasons.

_____

_____

_____

_____

Story update: *A diagnosis is not a defect!*

Let's meet Mike. Mike's parents left early for work, so he was always the last one out of the house in the morning. He had a routine that was pretty simple—fill the water dish for the cat, turn off the lights, turn off the coffee machine, lock the door, and run to meet the bus. While on the bus this morning, the thought popped in his head that maybe he had left the coffee machine on. *That doesn't even really keep coffee hot. Nothing to worry about*, he thought. But then, images of fire started spreading through his mind as he imagined it spreading through his home. He texted his mom, who quickly reassured him that the coffee machine turns off automatically after a while anyway. But throughout the day, the images of his home burning, his cat suffering, his family and community blaming him, his life being ruined, just kept hammering him.

All was fine in the end, but the next morning, Mike got up extra early to make time for a more elaborate check of the necessary items. He walked from each item to the next while saying aloud: "This is done, I see that it's done." That seemed to help, for a few days anyway, until the images of catastrophe starting intruding in class. This time, the image involved a light bulb shorting out and bursting into flames. The next day, he added to his checking routine by turning the lights off, then on, then off, then on again to make sure that they were working properly and then definitely off.

This addition to his routine seemed to relieve his distress for some time until he started worrying about whether the door was locked. Images of burglars invaded his mind as he imagined them invading his home. He pictured his parents yelling at him for his incompetence as they showed him all the empty spots where prized possessions had once been. He pictured his cat wandering around the neighborhood, desperate for food, cold, confused because, of course, the burglars let him out. *Now the routine needs a strategy for guaranteeing the doors are certainly locked*, he thought.

Fast-forward a week or two and Mike needs fifteen minutes to lock, unlock, relock, take pictures of, and make the right statements about the front and back door of his house. He hates it, but if he doesn't get it feeling just right, he can't function at school, his mind helplessly devoted to telling stories about how one mistake ruined everything. Some days his mind wouldn't let him feel finished enough, so he would miss the bus and make up excuses, like saying he was sick that day. Some days he would try to get his parents to come home from work early to make sure he hadn't made a mistake. Some days he would text them confessing that he thought he forgot something, demanding they tell him specifically, "You got everything." He often had difficulty concentrating at school. *Who cares if I understand the American Revolution if my house is burning down?* he would think. Grades started to slip, and so did sleep. He would lie awake at night planning his checking rituals, thinking this time they would guarantee freedom from thoughts about it the next day.

for you to do

Mike seems to fit the bill for an OCD diagnosis. He has obsessions, compulsions, and disorder. You may or may not share Mike's traits (other activities in this book may identify your specific theme or content), but see if you can identify specifically what makes his story an OCD story:

Obsessions are unwanted, intrusive thoughts. What obsessions does Mike have?

_____

_____

_____

Compulsions are physical or mental behaviors designed to reduce distress or feel more certain about obsessions. What compulsions do you think Mike is engaging in?

_____

_____

_____

Disorder is a word used to suggest that there are ways in which the symptoms (obsessions and compulsions) make life especially challenging. How do Mike's symptoms make his life harder?

_____

_____

_____

more to do

Now that you have an idea of how to identify obsessions, compulsions, and disorder, use the space below to break down your own OCD symptoms. You may fit squarely into one theme (we'll go into themes in the pages ahead), or your OCD may like to go in a lot of different directions. Jot down a few examples of what comes up for you. What are you afraid of happening? What is hard for you to accept uncertainty about? What thoughts run away with you?

My symptoms include:

_____

_____

_____

_____

List some of the compulsions you engage in to deal with these obsessions. These could include physical behaviors (such as checking or washing), mental behaviors (reviewing scenes or ideas over and over in your head), and things like asking other people for reassurance or avoiding anything that triggers your unwanted thoughts.

My compulsions include:

_____

_____

_____

_____

What about those obsessions and compulsions lead you to believe that there is a disorder to address? Does your experience of these symptoms cause you to miss out on things, feel poorly about yourself, interfere in concentration and enjoyment of life?

This disorder interferes with my life because:

_____

_____

_____

_____

_____

It may have been difficult to write that. Deciding it's time to stand up to your OCD and take back what it's taken from you requires a lot of courage. Take this opportunity to write down some things you think you will reclaim when you get mastery over OCD. What experiences do you want to have once you've achieved freedom from OCD?

_____

_____

_____

_____

_____

_____

_____

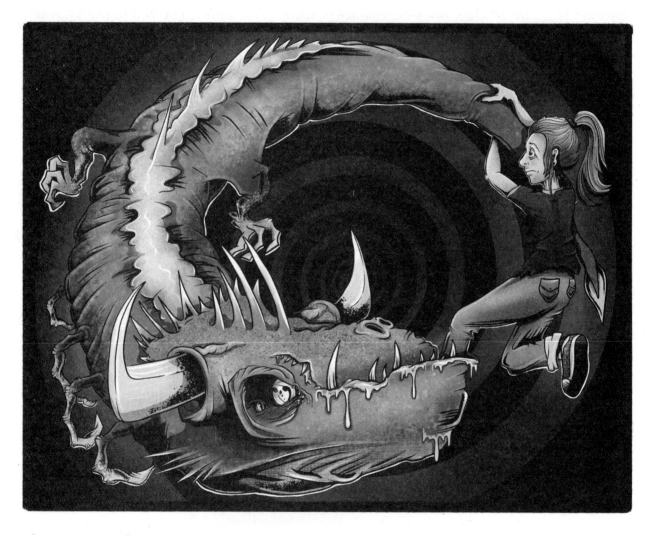

Story update: *Obsessions are unwanted thoughts and compulsions are responses to those thoughts that get us stuck in a loop.*

for you to know

OCD is considered a biopsychosocial disorder, which means it has biological, psychological, and social roots. Biologically, we know that OCD probably has a genetic component to it, that it often runs in families, and that if you have OCD, you are a lot more likely than the average person to have a family member with a similar disorder. We also know that how you relate psychologically to your unwanted thoughts impacts how they seem to you. And on the social front, well, you're at an age where you're starting to be introduced to some new concepts about life that previously might not have been so interesting. Sex, romantic love, religion, violence—these are all issues that teens are suddenly expected to "get," when just a few years ago the idea of a tooth fairy seemed perfectly reasonable. In short, teens are often hit hard with OCD symptoms because the brain is growing new tools for information processing *and* the world is asking you to process a lot of new information.

Sarah hated health class. The school had decided it was time everyone should know about safe sex and healthy pregnancy this semester, but nobody had asked her! She didn't like to think about these things because, when she did, the images she associated with the subject seemed to stick around in her head all day. It wasn't just the pictures and diagrams of genitals, fallopian tubes, and uteruses (that was gross enough), but the fact that the whole discussion of the sexual body and how it works seemed to make her think of people she knew having sex. She'd look over at her friend at the next desk and suddenly be bombarded with images of her friend performing sex acts. Same when she looked at the teacher, an old frumpy man with a giant mole on his nose. The effects of the class seemed to follow her everywhere, so that even at the dinner table she had to fight with herself to find a way to distract herself from picturing her family members having sex! She often wondered if she was doing something wrong by having these thoughts, if they meant she wanted to perform disgusting sex acts with people. It wasn't long ago that she never thought about sex at all. Maybe she'd make her stuffed animals kiss and that would mean they were married now. Suddenly, everything was penises and vaginas, and she hated it and hated herself for thinking about it. She tried her best to replace the unwanted thoughts with wholesome, wanted thoughts, but this never provided more than a minute's relief and always resulted in her unwanted thoughts being even more intrusive.

for you to do

Sarah's OCD presents as unwanted sexual thoughts and she tried to replace them with "good" thoughts, but this compulsion didn't really work. It's likely she had OCD before her health class brought this theme to her attention. But it's also possible she didn't notice any OCD symptoms until just now, and that's why she just *assumed* something was morally wrong with her.

Take a moment to consider what kinds of new experiences or new material you've been exposed to since you became a teenager. Write them down here.

_____

_____

_____

_____

Can you identify any themes that suddenly seem important for you to be certain about? This could be anything, really. Sarah was newly exposed to the subject of sex, but what about all the other stuff you didn't think of as a little kid? Diseases, acts of violence, dating, college, career, the meaning of life …?

_____

_____

_____

_____

more to do

One of the things that gets in the way of tackling OCD is the assumption that you must be doing something wrong, or failing in some way for having these symptoms. Notice how Sarah blamed herself for struggling with stuck thoughts after health class. But obviously it's not her fault for having OCD, for having to go to health class, and for having her OCD turn health class into a nightmare for her. Use the space below to explain how having your theme isn't necessarily your fault.

_____

_____

_____

_____

Story update: *Having OCD is not your fault and being a teen comes with plenty of its own challenges.*

4 the deal with intrusive thoughts

for you to know

For the rest of this workbook, you're going to be focusing on your least favorite subject (no, not chemistry): your intrusive thoughts. An intrusive thought is like any other intruder. It shows up at the party uninvited, brings nothing for your guests, complains about the music, double-dips in the salsa, and spills punch on your parents' carpet. Let's get to know the *intrusive thought*.

Intrusive thoughts don't happen because you did something wrong or because you're some kind of messed-up person. They're actually a normal part of the human experience. Everyone has intrusive thoughts. People with OCD are more likely to view their intrusive thoughts as problematic and feel like they have a responsibility to do something about them.

Intrusive thoughts are like internet spammers. For example, I have a bunch of followers on my social media that I know are not really my friends or my fans. They're fake accounts used to market something. I get a lot of friend requests or follows from people who are obvious bots, just computer programs designed to look like people to boost their numbers or sell me stuff.

Most of my online platforms have a filtering system that weeds out the junk mail and bots without me having to pay any attention to it. Occasionally I have to take a look and decide for myself. It's not that hard because I know really, really good-looking people with nothing but ads in their posts are suspicious. Emails from people who think I am a safe place to temporarily hold their wealth, if only they had my bank info and Social Security number, are spam.

No filtering system is perfect, and the one in your head that filters out intrusive thoughts doesn't always catch the obvious bots. Sometimes you have to explore them before tagging them as junk and rejecting them, but most of the time you can recognize junk without looking very hard. Learning to overcome OCD is basically just learning to program your mental filter to be more effective.

As I mentioned before, an obsession is an unwanted, intrusive thought that shows up in your mind and feels like something you need to get rid of. Another good way to understand the intrusive thought is that it's like any other thought, except that it seems to have a quality to it that feels impossible to accept uncertainty about.

Here are some things people with OCD commonly struggle to accept uncertainty about:

- germs or chemicals and whether they will get you or others sick

- violent thoughts and whether they predict violent behaviors

- mistakes with tragic consequences and whether you've checked things carefully enough

- moral intentions and whether yours are good

- sexual attractions and whether yours are normal or fit your identity

- relationships and whether you're in the right one

- responsibilities and whether you've done everything you're supposed to do

- health and whether yours is in good shape

- religious concerns and whether you're doing right by your faith

- philosophical concerns and the meaning of life

- sanity and whether yours is intact

- discomfort, incompleteness, imperfection, or disgust and whether what you're experiencing will ever go away

- attention and whether yours is stuck on something it shouldn't be

for you to do

That list doesn't cover every thought a person could struggle to accept uncertainty about, of course. Anything can be an obsession. Use the space below to jot down other thoughts a person might struggle with.

_____

_____

_____

_____

_____

_____

_____

_____

_____

more to do

Everybody experiences intrusive thoughts, but you have a special kind of mind that picks up intrusive thoughts like a big satellite. It's kind of like you were born with the deluxe cable package in your head. It comes with Nickelodeon, some music channels, all the sports channels, HBO, Showtime, and a few hundred channels you never watch—plus a few channels you wish you didn't have. The downside to this is that you end up seeing things you'd rather not see when you surf for something to watch. But the upside is that you occasionally see pretty cool things that you'd never go out of your way to look for.

Take a moment to consider whether people have ever called you creative or funny, or asked you how you came up with something. The same type of mind that presents you with "out there" stuff you *don't* want also presents you with "out there" stuff that makes you stand out in a *good* way. Use the space below to jot down a few examples of ways in which your unique mind has made you stand out in a good way, the way that makes people say, "Wow, how did you come up with that?" or "Wow, that is so you" and mean it as a compliment.

_____

_____

_____

_____

_____

_____

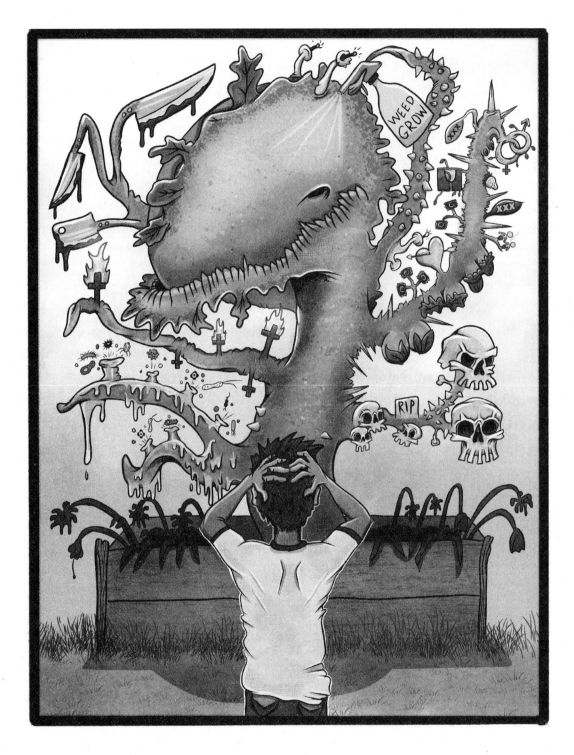

Story update: *Part of being a big thinker is being creative, even when you don't want to!*

the deal with compulsions 5

for you to know

Treating OCD is not rocket science. OCD wants one thing: for you to do compulsions. You want to stop compulsions and starve the OCD out. The key to beating OCD is to get really good at recognizing what a compulsion is and then abandoning it, *choosing uncertainty instead*. As you probably already know, the way to get good at something is to practice it. So first we need to recognize what a compulsion is, then we have to bring up the urge to do the compulsion, and *then* we can practice rolling through the urge *without* doing a compulsion. When you resist compulsions, it can feel really intense, scary, or disgusting. Your OCD assumes you will give in at the first sight of these feelings, so it dumps them on you whenever you defy it. You are using this workbook to prove it wrong.

A compulsion is a behavior, something you do to reduce the distress you feel when you have an intrusive thought or feeling. This behavior can be physical, as in repeatedly washing your hands, or mental, as in analyzing a thought until it feels right. It can be avoidant, as in trying not to see or touch something triggering, or repetitive, as in going back multiple times to check that the door is locked. It can be entirely private, as in secretly counting to a safe number in your head, or involve others, as in asking questions for reassurance.

To learn to catch and resist compulsions is simply to ask what message you want to send to your brain about the situation you are in. Before you can pull this off, you can start tracking your triggers (what's bothering you) and your compulsive responses (what you are doing to address these triggers).

for you to do

To get a clear picture of what you're doing and what you need to change to beat the OCD, start a log of your triggers and how you're responding to them. You can do this any way you like: in a small notebook, on your phone or device if you have one, or with the form below. You don't have to log every single experience. The point *is not* to overwhelm yourself with data. The point *is* to get a decent idea of what's really going on. You're getting triggered. You're responding to those triggers. Something in that response is sending the signal to your brain that you're in danger or that something bad is going to happen. Once you can see that, you can design a plan to start sending a different signal. Try a few entries now based on what you've experienced today.

Trigger (what set me off)	Response (what I did)

You can download this template at http://www.newharbinger.com/46363 and practice using it daily.

more to do

Take a piece of paper or something like it and cover the "trigger" column of your log. Take a look at the responses only. If you didn't know what triggers led to the response, what would you think about whatever caused the responses? For example, if the response was "washed hands," and you didn't know what the trigger was, a reasonable assumption would be that your hands were dirty. Or if the response was "asked for reassurance that I'm a good person," and you didn't know what the trigger was, you might assume that you were unsure whether you were a good person in that moment. These assumptions are the signals your brain gets from the behaviors you're struggling to resist right now. Use the space below to identify what assumptions your brain is probably making based on your compulsions.

_____

_____

_____

_____

_____

_____

Now use the space below to write down what it is you actually *want* your brain to know instead. For example, you *want* your brain to know that your hands are clean and that you truly are a good person. You *want* your brain to know that the things you're afraid of are no big deal, are things you can handle. You actually have a really cool brain. It's not your enemy. It's just that right now you're using strategies for operating this cool brain that make it more likely to glitch. To get your brain on board here, you have to *show* it by using different behaviors than the ones that teach it to be afraid. Understanding what you want your brain to know will help you figure out which behaviors to choose when you're ready to start making changes.

Story update: *Compulsions strengthen the OCD by teaching the brain to be afraid.*

6 mental rituals: having thoughts vs. messing around with thoughts

for you to know

In the past, people who treated OCD used to rely on a lot of mental games, like asking you to try to replace an unwanted thought with one you liked or using different strategies for arguing logically with your fears to prove they're not true. We now understand that not only do these strategies not work, but they also often make you worse. Why? Because they're also compulsions and, as you probably figured out in the last activity, compulsions send the wrong signal to your brain. Compulsions that others cannot see, that occur in the mind, are called mental rituals. If you get good at catching and abandoning *these* trolls, you definitely get the upper hand on your OCD.

Hey, just a heads-up, this next bit might creep you out a little. Just remember this is a workbook for learning something and sometimes learning is gross. I remember dissecting a frog in science class. Gross, but on the upside I guess I know frogs inside and out.

Jordan was babysitting his little sister while his parents went out for a date night. Everything was going fine, despite him being bored watching her play the same stupid video game over and over. He decided it was time for dinner, so he microwaved her a hot dog and then started cutting it up into bite-size pieces the way she liked it. Even though he felt uncool about it, he liked his sister and he kind of liked the responsibility his parents trusted him with in babysitting her.

Then, seemingly out of nowhere, Jordan looked at the knife. In his mind, the image of him plunging it into his sister flashed. It was super detailed. Impressive special effects, if you get my drift. Bloody and realistic, not CGI. He almost jumped it frightened him so much. Jordan didn't want to hurt his sister. He wasn't the sort to want to really hurt anyone. He'd never even been in a fistfight. But because this horrific image was so vivid and so contrary to anything he would normally think, it was immediately followed by a series of questions, both impossible to answer and impossible to resist trying to answer.

Why did I have this thought? Would I ever do such a thing? How do I know it's safe for me to be around my sister? What would people think of me if they knew I had this thought? Is it safe for me to be holding this knife right now? What are all the reasons I would never hurt my sister? Are there any reasons I would? Are any events in my past clues as to why I might be a secret murderer? Should I avoid my violent video games and movies? Why do I like those anyway? What kind of a sicko am I? What's to stop me from stabbing my sister? What about other people I love? What about anyone?

He tried to answer each and every one of these questions, but the answers were never good enough and always led to more questions. All the while, this image of him stabbing his sister persisted and was now joined with images of stabbing anyone else who popped up in his mind. He tried to replace the "stabbing" image with a "helping" image, but that didn't work. He tried replaying the scene with a different happy ending over and over, but that didn't work. He tried repeating comforting phrases like "I love my sister" and "I would never do that" but that didn't work. He tried distracting himself by doing math problems, but … guess what?

for you to do

Jordan's in a bit of pickle. He wants to make the bad thoughts go away, but the strategies he's using seem not to work. Actually, they seem to be making things worse. Jordan is engaging in *mental rituals* and the thing about mental rituals is they often just look like regular thinking or figuring out your problems. When treating people with OCD, we *never* tell them to try not to think their unwanted thoughts. If that worked, why would you need this workbook and why would I even have a job? But we *do* ask that you try to recognize when your thinking about your unwanted thoughts is compulsive.

Thinking is something we *do,* like eating or sleeping. We don't always know when we're doing it, but it is a thing we *do,* not a thing that just happens to us. Thoughts are just words or images that pop up in our heads. Understanding the difference between *thinking* (a behavior) and *having thoughts* (an experience) is a big part of understanding OCD and how to overcome it.

Mental rituals are the things you do in your head to try to prove to yourself that your fears won't come true, or to try to be certain that you understand your thoughts perfectly. Here are a few worth remembering:

- *Ruminating*—digging up an unwanted thought and replaying or analyzing it over and over to try to be more certain about it. Interesting side note: When cows eat grass and stuff, it first goes into one compartment of the stomach and sits there. Later they literally puke it up into their mouths and chew it again to better digest it, and then swallow it again. This process is *also* called ruminating. Kinda funny because mental ruminating is like throwing up your thoughts to try to digest them again. You're welcome. (Insert puke emoji.)

- *Mental checking*—going back to a thought to make sure it's still there, or gone, or is addressed right

- *Thought neutralizing*—trying to replace or block a thought you don't like with one you do like

- *Rationalizing*—going over and over in your head all the reasons why you don't need to worry about your unwanted thoughts

- *Self-reassurance*—telling yourself over and over that your fears are unlikely to happen, or repeatedly reminding yourself of comforting things you've heard about your fears

How did Jordan use these mental rituals to try to be more certain about his unwanted thought?

_____

_____

_____

How do you use these mental rituals?

_____

_____

_____

There are countless ways to use your mind to do compulsions. Can you think of others? You can also make up names for ruminating, mental checking, and thought neutralizing that are totally your invention. For example, ruminating is kind of like getting caught in an OCD spiderweb, so you could call it *Spidermanning* if you want. Use the space below to make up names for your mental rituals. Totally your call what the names are.

_____

_____

_____

_____

more to do

You may have heard the expression "knowing is half the battle." It's not really true. Knowing is like 10 percent of the battle, tops. Making choices and following through with them is what makes up the other 90 percent. The trick to beating mental rituals is hard but simple.

1. Label the mental ritual. You can use the ones I mentioned earlier in the chapter and/or the ones you came up with.

2. Abandon the mental ritual. By "abandon," I mean immediately jump out of the thought process and get back to what you were paying attention to before your mind wandered into the ritual.

This "label and abandon" technique is not easy. Your OCD has had lots of practice roping you into mental rituals, and you're just now starting to learn to catch, name, and abandon them. So don't expect it to make a huge difference immediately. Just start practicing from this point forward, and every time you catch a mental ritual and let go of it, even for just a moment, give yourself a thumbs-up. This is part of *mindfulness*, and it's a good thing to practice, whether it lasts or not.

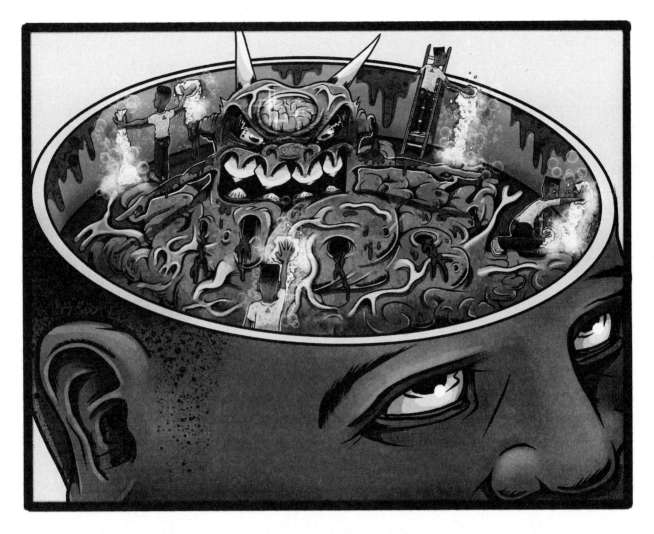

Story update: *Thinking is an activity, like washing, and we can catch and abandon it.*

7 mindfulness: boss level boredom

for you to know

Whatever obsession you're currently stuck on, one thing is clear—you are consumed by a story, but it doesn't feel that way. If you watch a cool movie, the same thing happens. You forget for a second that it's just actors and makeup and special effects. You can almost forget that it's not real and it's taking place in outer space or the Old West. So when your favorite character dies, you feel sad. When someone falls in love, you feel moved. When something blows up, you feel excited. But why? Nothing actually happened to *you*. The answer is simply that you forgot, just for a moment, that you're just a person sitting in a chair looking at a screen full of lights and listening to sounds. You thought, just for a second, that you were in the movie. This is a lot of fun when we do it by choice, not so much when the movie is directed by OCD. Mindfulness, put simply, is just remembering the truth, being aware that everything we experience involves our five senses and our thoughts, and that a story is not the same thing as a reality. It's okay if the word "mindfulness" immediately makes you bored. I felt the same way for a really long time. Hear me out.

All this stuff you're learning is pretty cool as long as you are fully aware of what you're doing. But we spend an awful lot of time on autopilot just going from one thing to the next without really being aware of it. How many times do you read a class assignment and get to the bottom of the page only to realize that, although you looked at the words, you really spent the time thinking about something else? So improving our attention and increasing our awareness makes it harder for OCD to trick us. For this, we need this thing I've been hinting at since the beginning—mindfulness.

"Cool, cool, cool, but how do I get this mythical awareness you speak of?" you may ask. First, think of everything you find even the least bit entertaining, and then stop doing it. Okay, I'm at least half kidding. If you're anything like I used to be, the first thing that comes to mind when asked to put down your phone, stop your game, turn off your music, or shut down your computer is BOREDOM, dying a slow, painful death from boredom. This is because we spend almost every waking moment lost in a story. When a story displeases us even for a second, we just switch to another story. Try sitting in any waiting room for more than five seconds without picking up your electronic device. Don't have your device with you? How long does it take before you settle for a magazine?

When we get rid of all the stories, meaning, when we drop the things that tell us stories (our newsfeeds, games, conversations, and so on), we get to see what's left, what isn't a story. Because this almost never happens, our brains are conditioned to respond negatively to it. BOOOORING, let's get outta here. "Oh, here's a fake rocket launcher I can buy with fake money on a fake online game; thank goodness I have something to do now!" But what if you could approach this thing you call boredom in a different way? What happens when you look at the absence of distraction with curiosity instead of rejection? Let's find out.

for you to do

Find a quiet, private place to sit. You can sit in a chair or cross-legged on the floor, doesn't matter. Just make sure your back is supported so you can be basically upright and alert without straining much. You can read the following instructions enough times that you can commit them to memory, or you can go to http://www .newharbinger.com/46363 to listen to an audio version of this exercise:

1. Close your eyes and mentally ask how your body feels. What I mean is, ask yourself, *What does my foot feel like right now?* Maybe it's feeling pressure against the floor. *What does the weight of my body feel like? What do my hands feel like from the inside?* Of course, your mind is going to wander, and that's fine, but just try to keep bringing it back to this one question: *What am I sensing with my body?*

2. Do the exact same thing, but this time check what's going on in the world of sound. Are there any noises in the background? Can you hear yourself breathing? Listen carefully and pick out each individual sound as if they were tracks on an audio recording. Again, your attention will not be stable, but that's cool. Just keep coming back to this one question: *What am I hearing?*

3. Now bring your attention to your breathing. You've checked out your sensations and you've checked out sounds, and now you're going to look at something made up of both—your breathing in and your breathing out. Notice where you feel the air just barely start to enter your lungs. Notice where you feel your lungs to be full. Notice where you feel them empty. Of course, your mind will wander. When it does, just keep coming back to this one question: *Where is my breath?*

This thing you keep coming back to is called your *anchor*. Meditating can take many forms, but in its most basic form it is simply identifying an anchor, putting your attention on it, noticing when your attention wanders, and then coming back to it— no questions asked.

more to do

Okay, now that you have the basic idea of sitting, checking in with sensations, checking in with sound, and then locking in on your breath, let's give this meditation thing a try. Remember, all you have to do is try to bring your attention to your breath. Whenever you notice that you're paying attention to anything else, even your thoughts, just bring your attention back to your breath. Why? Because this is how you learn to tell the difference between what is a story (like the stuff your OCD thoughts are always telling you) and what is not a story (like you are a person sitting and breathing).

So set a timer for just a minute first. Pay attention to the experience of breathing and come back to your anchor whenever you wander off.

A minute later, how do you feel?

_____

_____

_____

Try the exercise again, this time for two minutes.

Two minutes later, how do you feel?

_____

_____

_____

Try the exercise once more, this time without timing it at all. See if you can notice the exact moment you start wondering how much longer you can take the boredom. See what happens when you keep going even longer than that. Does the boredom stay constant? Does it change?

Open your eyes whenever you've decided you've had enough. Use the space below to write down any ideas you have about this experience. Was it easy? Was it hard? What did you notice distracting you from your breath the most?

_____

_____

_____

_____

_____

_____

_____

You can use this exercise daily to practice this "bringing your attention back" skill. I also like to experiment with different guided meditations from different meditation teachers (shout-out to the Headspace and Ten Percent Happier apps, which I think are particularly cool).

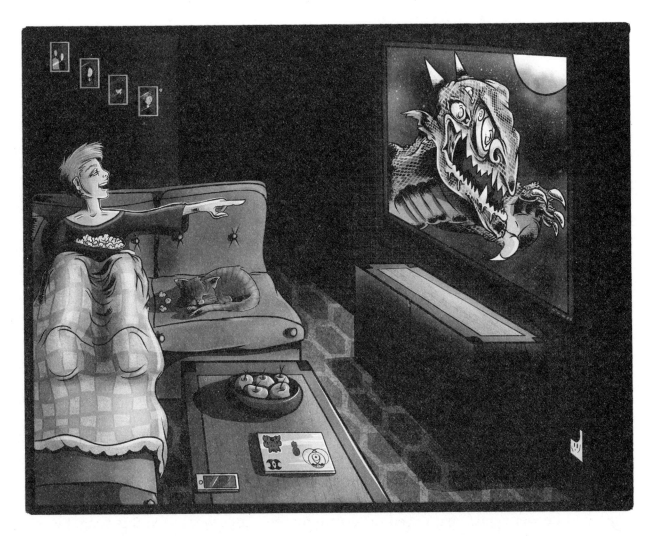

Story update: *If we reduce distractions, we can learn to watch our thoughts and pay a different kind of attention to them.*

8 making your own meditation games

for you to know

Mindfulness is about paying a different kind of attention to your experience. Traditional breathing meditation can train you to cultivate this kind of attention, but there are many ways to practice this even when you don't find the time to sit and meditate. All that's required is that you take anything you are used to experiencing and ask yourself to pay close attention to a particular part of it. Your mind will naturally gravitate back to what it's used to, and then you can practice inviting it to return to the idea of your choosing. Consider how this skill, of watching your mind do what it always does and then inviting it to attend to something of your choosing, can give you an advantage over your OCD.

I saw a YouTube video some time ago of a pop song with the bass guitar isolated. This was a song I'd heard many times, and a catchy one. Upon hearing the bass alone, I was pretty shocked at how I had never noticed it. This bass player was a master of his craft, and I never would've guessed in reverse that this bass went with this song. I was aware of the song, but not its individual parts.

Becoming more mindful is a lot like this. It means experiencing something in the present moment, but actually noticing individual textures in it, countless ways you can remain attuned to it. Think about how your OCD can rip you away from anything (like your homework, the movie you were just watching, the conversation you were having) and what a difficult time you have returning. Now that the OCD has your attention, it feels really weird to try to return from it to something simple like the present. But what if the present weren't so simple? Like that song, what if it was made up of individually noticeable, dynamic, and interesting parts? Then there would be a lot to return to, and whatever story your OCD is going on about would have some serious competition.

for you to do

Pick an object to be your meditation anchor for this exercise. By "object," I mean anything you could pay attention to. It could be a physical object, like a pen or an article of clothing, or you could use a song, a video, a drawing, or a piece of food.

What did you choose as your meditation anchor? (Example: *An apple*)

_____

What is the first thing you notice about it? (Example: *Its red color*)

_____

What was it before it became this thing? (Example: *A seed*)

_____

Will it always be this thing or could it change? How? (Example: *It could become applesauce.*)

_____

_____

What other senses can be used to experience this thing? (Example: *Smell, taste*)

_____

more to do

Whatever object (or image) you used for the exercise above, you know it better now than you did before. Now select one new thing you noticed about the object and focus your attention there. For the next two minutes (set a timer if you wish) try to keep your attention there. If your attention wanders, that's okay; just return it immediately to the detail you were focusing on. In other words, just like the apple's color stood out in the example I gave, use your mind to single out one aspect of the object and really pay attention to it. Again, your mind will wander because that's what minds do, so just notice when that happens and then return your attention. After the two minutes are up, write down what you experienced.

_____

_____

_____

_____

Story update: *Meditation is mostly just catching your mind wandering and choosing where to place your attention.*

9 challenging the way you think

for you to know

Mindfulness means remembering what you're actually doing, like remembering that when you're obsessing what you're doing is just thinking. Part of being aware that you're thinking is recognizing that there are styles of thinking that help and styles of thinking that make you really feel stuck having to do compulsions. These thinking styles are sometimes called *cognitive distortions*. If you can be aware of these thinking styles, you can challenge them, just by being aware.

Dave was super protective of his bedroom. Nothing from the outside world could enter the room unless it had been cleaned a very specific way. He was pretty sure some kids at his school did not wash their hands after using the toilet, which meant they were touching things at school with toilet hands. This meant the clothes he was wearing, his bookbag, and all his school supplies had toilet germs on them. He was very careful to touch as little as possible at school, but what really mattered to him was making sure nothing that was at school got into his bedroom.

When he got home, he would strip at the entrance and run to the shower. He would later do his homework at the kitchen table, and if he had to go to his room, he would wash up to his elbows before entering. If he touched the table where his homework was, his hands were dirty again, so he had to go wash if he needed to get anything from his room. He was sure that if he entered his room with "dirty" hands, the entire room would be contaminated and he would never feel clean enough to sleep again.

46

No one in his family could help because their way of washing wasn't good enough, so he had to wash anything he thought they touched as well. Sometimes he couldn't decide whether something had touched something that had been at school, but it just felt dirty somehow, so he would wash it anyway. In his most frustrating moments, he would be sitting in his room and start thinking about things being dirty, and then worry that this somehow made his bed unclean and he had to change the sheets because he strongly believed he should never sleep in a dirty bed.

for you to do

Here's a list of thinking styles that strengthen your OCD and make it hard to resist compulsions:

- *All-or-nothing*—assuming something is totally one way or totally the opposite

- *Catastrophizing*—assuming something bad will happen that you couldn't handle

- *Overestimating responsibility*—assuming everything you can think of is your fault

- *Magical thinking*—assuming what goes on in your head affects anything outside your head

- *Emotional reasoning*—assuming something is true because it feels that way

- *"Should" thinking*—assuming an inflexible rule about how things must be

Notice how all these thinking styles involve making *assumptions* about things you can't really know for certain.

Where do you see these thinking styles in Dave's story?

_____

_____

_____

Why do you think these styles of thinking are unhelpful?

_____

_____

_____

_____

more to do

Which thinking styles do you think push you to do compulsions? You can use the examples above or make up some of your own. The trick is to have names for the way you think so you can call them out.

_____

_____

_____

When you call out your thinking style, you can shift from *having* to do compulsions to being able to choose again. It might not be an easy choice, but catching your assumptions can really help. The really hard part is challenging the way you're thinking *without* arguing with your OCD. Arguing with your OCD often ends up with mental rituals (remember rumination and the other rituals in Activity 6?). But *challenging* a thought can help you turn away from compulsions. Check this out.

What got to me	What I thought	Challenge
Saw a red mark on my desk	I might have touched it and I have to wash or I'll get a disease and die!	I don't know if my hands are dirty or not. This feels like all-or-nothing and catastrophizing. Gonna leave this alone and take my chances, stand up to OCD.

Writing down and organizing your thoughts this way can be a good way of looking at the obsession from a different angle without getting lost in an OCD story. Just remember, we never get into the "math" of the problem. In other words, don't try to convince yourself of the probability your fear won't come true. Just challenge the thinking style and encourage yourself to resist compulsions. Try it for yourself:

What got to me	What I thought	Challenge

You can download this thought-challenging log at http://www.newharbinger
.com/46363 and practice this skill daily.

Story update: *Recognizing unhelpful ways of thinking can be useful for resisting compulsions.*

10 cool story, bruh: responding to unwanted thoughts

What does a bully actually want from you? Think about this for a second. Your lunch money, a sparring partner, the cheers of his henchmen—none of these really seem worth it. I suspect a bully's primary drive is knowing he got you to go from a peaceful state to a defensive one. What happens next is icing on the cake. The real prize is making you fight, not the fight itself.

OCD is just like this. It points out the things you find triggering and then tells you that it's your fault they're there and your job to do something about them. When you agree to this, you end up doing compulsions, hoping that that fulfills your responsibility and makes the triggers go away. But it's a trap. The moment you do that, the OCD says "Nyah-nyah, I got you" and the taunting, the demand for more compulsions, persists right after that.

Learning to respond to your OCD demands with a variety of nondefensive comebacks can be the key to getting this bully off your back. Here are four approaches:

- Ignore it. Literally pretend it isn't happening. Just keep doing what you were doing, even if the bully is pouring a milkshake over your head while you study. Just wipe the milkshake off your brow and keep studying.

- Acknowledge it, but don't respond. This approach is mindful, relating to the OCD like you might relate to any distraction that came up while meditating. You would note that the OCD is there, but then return to what you were focusing on before you got distracted.

- Agree that it might be right and you don't really care. This would mean taking what the bully is saying and responding with a variation of "Yup, could be" and "Cool story, bruh."

- Agree completely and make things uncomfortable for the bully. This would mean taking what the OCD is saying, commenting that it's "so true," and then one-upping it by saying something way worse.

for you to do

Take the four approaches listed in the last section and write out a response that applies to your OCD. Start by writing an example of something your OCD might say. It might be something like "You may have touched someone's urine in the restroom and not completely washed it off."

What would ignoring that really look like?

_____

_____

What would you say to yourself to acknowledge that you heard what the OCD had to say, but didn't plan to do anything about it?

_____

_____

What would you say or do if you wanted to suggest that what the OCD was going on about _could_ be true, but that you weren't particularly impressed?

_____

_____

What would be an example of "yes, and _also_" that would be so absurd that the OCD could only come back with "You're weird, I'm outta here!"? So if the OCD says you're going to get contaminated by something, you might say, "Yeah, right up my nose and into my brain!"

_____

_____

Remember, it's not about finding the perfect response to your thoughts. Use whatever works, but follow this one rule—_never_ defend yourself from the OCD. Don't let it pick that fight!

more to do

Take a moment to reflect on these different responses and make some notes here about how each response works for you. They each come with pros and cons. Ignoring is certainly low-maintenance, but can feel a bit too much like avoidance. Agreeing can bring some humor and bravado into the equation, but it can also spike your anxiety at an inconvenient time. Which do you think you're going to use the most and why?

_____

_____

_____

_____

_____

_____

Story update: *There is no one perfect way to respond to OCD—except never playing defense!*

electronic rap punk (ERP) 11

for you to know

Okay, so I made you look. ERP doesn't stand for electronic rap punk, but it does involve dancing to your own beat, thinking quickly and creatively with words, and being loud and subversive, so there's that. ERP stands for *exposure and response prevention*, which is the best known treatment we have for OCD. In Activity 5, I mentioned that the key to beating OCD is to identify and choose not to do compulsions. If you're going to get good at this (and you will), you need to practice wanting to do compulsions and then staying in that space between being triggered and giving in. *Exposure* just means purposely doing the things that bring on that urge to do compulsions. *Response prevention* just means not doing them. Why bother? Because this is how you teach your brain that it *can* handle this.

Maybe you've heard about ERP, and the idea makes you throw up in your mouth a bit. I don't blame you. There's a lot of bad info out there about this kind of therapy. Let me quickly get out in front of some of the misinformation.

- **ERP is not torture.** It's funny when people trip over things—that's just objectively true—but it's not funny when they get seriously hurt, and for no reason. Choosing to do exposures to your fears is going to hurt, but the *hurting* part of it is not the reason to do it. Otherwise, it *would* be torture. Choosing to do exposure to your fears is all about challenging yourself to win back what your OCD has taken from you and to bulk up the muscles needed to keep the OCD from ripping you off again.

- **ERP is not about forcing yourself to do things that you think are demeaning, demoralizing, or humiliating.** If you have to force yourself to expose to your fears, it doesn't really work. The OCD "knows" your heart's not really in it. Beating OCD in this game means *choosing* to do the hard things and feel the hard feelings because you understand how this works.

- **ERP is not about proving your fears won't come true or testing your reactions to your triggers.** Proving and testing compulsions are what got the OCD so revved up in the first place. ERP is about getting in that space between what triggers you and your compulsions and *learning* that you can handle the uncertainty and the feelings that come with it.

- **ERP is not about doing dangerous things or things that are likely to lead to harm coming to you or anyone else.** Learning to accept uncertainty involves rebuilding confidence in your abilities, and building confidence always means doing things you actually *want to do* and, er, not dying.

for you to do

A helpful way to get started with ERP is building what's called a hierarchy, which is just a list of ways you can defy the OCD, in order from easiest to hardest. Let's start coming up with the items that will go on that list. For this activity, we'll just focus on what is called *in vivo* exposures (we'll explore other types of exposures in the activities ahead). This means exposures you can do in real life—in other words, triggering things you can interact with, touch, watch, or listen to; things you can physically do; and places you can go to.

Use the worksheet below to write out all the exposures you could do in vivo that your OCD says you can't do. Remember, for every exposure, there also needs to be response prevention. Exposure is *defying* the OCD when it tells you that you can't do something, and response prevention is *denying* the OCD the satisfaction of seeing you do compulsions.

Use the left column to write out what you can do to egg on the OCD, and the right column to identify the compulsions you're going to resist. If you have a fear of contamination, an exposure might be touching the sink in your bathroom and the response prevention might be resisting washing your hands. If you have a fear of violent thoughts, an exposure might be going to the hunting section of a sporting goods store and the response prevention might be resisting the urge to ask for reassurance that you wouldn't do something harmful with a knife. For this exercise, just focus on what you are willing to try *today*.

Exposure (how I *defy* OCD)	Response Prevention (what I *deny* the OCD)

This worksheet is available at http://www.newharbinger.com/46363, and you can use it to repeatedly practice standing up to your OCD. It will change over time as you dominate the OCD by practicing your exposures again and again. Just keep printing new worksheets and updating your battle plan on the march to victory!

more to do

Starting off small is a good thing. True story: I learned how to ride a bike on a hand-me-down that had no brakes. I remember coasting down the hill of my parents' front yard (I must've been five or six) and then just bailing into the grass before I got to the street. Is this why I am the way I am? We'll never know. But for *you*, let's start smart. Take another look at the list you created above. These are things you believe you are ready to do today to stand up to your OCD. Now try to picture yourself actually doing these things. Picture engaging in the exposure, feeling the feelings this brings up, *watching* those feelings mindfully, and then *choosing* not to do compulsions (not holding your breath and waiting for it to end).

If 1 is the easiest and 10 is the hardest you can imagine, write a number next to each item on your list that represents the difficulty level. If they're all coming up 10s, it means you need to try to write the above exercise again with less demanding challenges. It is *absolutely okay* to make your first challenges so easy they make sense only to *you*. For example, if you're afraid of being contaminated by poison, and holding a closed canister of bug spray without immediately washing seems overwhelming, what about just touching the canister with one finger? Still a 10? What about touching a piece of paper that touched the bug spray? If that's a 9, how about just looking at the word "poison" or even the letter *P*? Try to get a few exposures in there that are in the 1 to 5 range, and always remember, an exposure is going to be effective only if you're *also* down for the response prevention (resisting compulsions).

Once you have a short list of challenges to do today that are varied in difficulty, start with the easiest ones and see how it goes. If you don't feel ready to do the harder ones after tackling some of the less challenging ones, that's cool too—not a problem. But if you do tackle the hardest ones, see if you can challenge yourself to do them all again but *this* time in a random order instead of easiest to hardest. Randomizing your exposures is a good way to create *generalization*, which means you're not just learning how to handle each individual trigger, but how to handle *being triggered* in general.

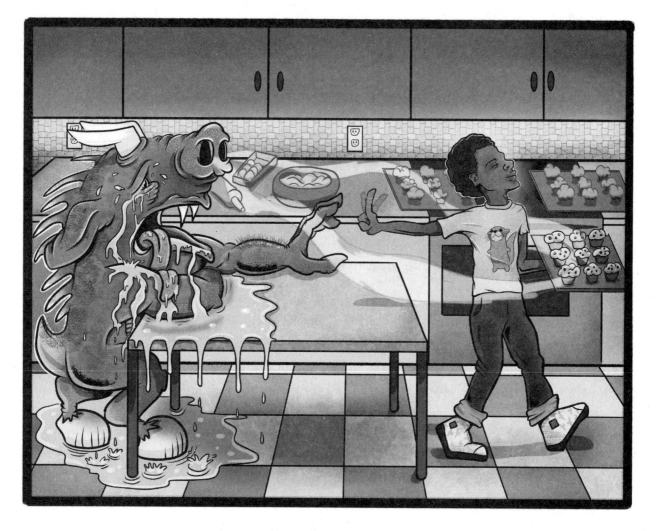

Story update: *Exposure is defying the OCD and response prevention is denying the OCD what it wants.*

you're a better writer than OCD 12

for you to know

In the previous activity, we explored in vivo ERP, or exposure and response prevention where you stand up to what triggers you in real life. But many obsessions involve thoughts that go way beyond anything that we can directly confront here on Earth. If you have fears that can't be confronted with in vivo ERP alone, or even if you do but want to defy the OCD in more than one way (OCD hates that), writing stories as a form of exposure can be really useful. This concept is usually called *imaginal ERP* or *scripting*.

When I was teenager, nerds like me read horror novels instead of playing horror video games. We would've played horror video games, but aside from contemplating what it would be like to run from edible ghosts in a perpetual maze, PAC-MAN didn't quite cut it. I particularly enjoyed stories with really graphic descriptions of mangled and mutated monster-people. Stories like these may not be your thing, but the writing was good and they made an impact on me. OCD fancies itself a horror novelist too. Its big dream is to have one of its scary stories made into a movie. Writing imaginal exposures, or scripting, is a great way to give your OCD a chance to pitch its story so, frankly, it can shut up about it.

for you to do

Writing out the scary story of your obsession is not just an exposure exercise. It's also a mindfulness exercise. By getting the thoughts out in front of you, on paper or on your computer, you're repositioning yourself as the observer. You're *looking at* the thoughts and seeing them as creations of the mind. Consider how reading a description of a nightmare is a different experience from actually having a nightmare and how describing it changes how you remember experiencing it.

Another way scripting helps is by letting you see the *whole* story of the obsession. One of the things that makes a monster in a horror movie so scary is that for most of the movie you see only little bits of it. Maybe a claw reaches out from behind something, or you see the monster's teeth in a jump-scare. By the time the full monster is revealed, it's usually not that scary anymore. Once you see the monster's tail attached to its body attached to its head, it's more of a special-effects spectacle than a terror inducer. So writing an imaginal exposure script is basically describing your monster from its head to the tip of its tail. You can try your hand at script writing by filling out the statements below. I've given you the option to use uncertainty language (may, might, could) or affirmative language (am, will, do, and so on). Different people have different ways of responding to language, and there's no exact right way to do this exercise, so just remember that we're trying to bring on the fear, and pick whichever language style gives you more goose bumps:

I am/have/will/may (write down your fear/obsession here) _____.

Because of this, I may/will (insert the worst immediate outcome of your fear being

true) _____. This could/will cause me to (insert a description

of how you are impacted negatively) _____.

People I care about might/will (insert a description of how others are negatively

affected by your fear coming true) _____.

This may/will lead me to (insert the worst possible thing that could happen next)

_____ and (go ahead and describe something even

worse than that) _____. Ultimately, I (insert a

description of having to cope with the fear being true in its worst way and/or going on

indefinitely—be brutal) _____.

Yikes! You really went there! Impressive! OCD can be brutal, but remember, this is
your life, not OCD's. Using your natural creativity skills to go bigger, bolder, even *sicker*
than the OCD is the way to mastery.

more to do

The purpose of an imaginal ERP script is the same as any ERP: to create that space between your triggering thoughts and your compulsions so you can practice being there without giving in to the OCD. So once you have a tight script that reflects what your OCD has been blabbing on about, read through it and ask yourself whether it generates the kind of distress other exposures do. If it doesn't, see if you can beef up the language with more detailed descriptions, or make the tone of the writing more aggressive or disturbing. Be creative and dramatic, but not so much that your script becomes too silly to generate discomfort. Remember, the goal is to purposefully feel what the OCD says you can't stand feeling!

Once you have a script that reliably excites the OCD, you can practice exposing to it while resisting doing compulsions. This type of ERP can be especially useful for practicing resisting mental rituals. As you read the script multiple times, you'll probably notice that you will get bored, start analyzing whether the fear really would come true or not, and maybe try to reassure yourself. Aim to resist all this. Fight the boredom by *trying* to get upset with what you're reading. Counter the analysis by repeatedly refocusing on the words you're exposing to. Block the self-reassurance by repeatedly noting, *Yep, this could happen, could be true, yes indeed.*

Try it now if you're up for it. Read your script ten times in a row with no breaks. Go slowly. Rushing sends the signal to your brain that this is something to avoid. We want to send the opposite signal! If your mind wanders, that's okay; just keep returning to the script. The script is your anchor in the same way that your breath is the anchor when you meditate—just this is, y'know, like, an evil meditation.

You can download the template from this activity at http://www.newharbinger .com/46363 and use it to make exposure scripts for all your OCD stories. Sometimes when we do exposure to a scary OCD story, the part that scares us the most can shift or change. Not a problem! Just modify the script to go where the OCD goes.

Story update: *Imaginal exposures are ways to use your creative writing skills to outwit the OCD.*

13 let's get physical (eww, sorry not sorry)

for you to know

So we've explored in vivo ERP and we've explored imaginal ERP. In other words, we looked at how you can defy the OCD with behaviors and defy the OCD with language. In this activity, you'll learn how to defy the OCD with your body itself. *Interoceptive* ERP means exposing yourself to the way it *feels in your body* to be triggered. For some types of obsessions, especially fears about body states, this may be the most direct way to target the OCD. This style of ERP can also be a good way to practice sitting with your unique experience of discomfort.

Ricardo was convinced he was losing his mind. He kept getting these random thoughts in his head about saying inappropriate or vulgar things in public. Often when he was in a group of people he would think, *I'm going to stand up and shout at the top of my lungs that I ...* and then whatever came next was something he would never say in a million years, something that would surely get him in trouble, humiliated, beat up, or imprisoned. Sometimes the thing he imagined blurting out was racist, sometimes sexually explicit, sometimes about hurting people, sometimes about there being a bomb in the building or an imminent school shooting. Sometimes he thought he might just start barking like a dog or speaking gibberish. He never actually said or did any of these things, of course, but the longer he worried about this obsession, the more it seemed like the words were right on the tip of his tongue.

To reassure himself that he wasn't going to snap, he tried really hard to monitor his body and keep it calm and still. He would also tell himself over and over, *You are in control.* If he noticed any signs of anxiety, he worried that might lead to him being impulsive, so he'd try to practice deep breathing exercises over and over, hoping no one would notice. If he started to feel warm, he worried that meant he was slipping into the danger zone, so he'd roll up his sleeves or fan himself with a piece of paper. *Calm and cool. Calm and cool*, he'd think. He would also compulsively cling to his chair or desk to try to stay centered, fearing that if he felt "off" or dizzy at any point, he might let some dangerous comment slip from his lips. Ricardo's OCD kept him trapped in a loop of trying not to feel things in order to make himself more certain that he wouldn't do something bad.

for you to do

Ricardo's OCD is a jerk. Can you imagine someone telling you what bodily sensations to have? We wouldn't tolerate this from anyone outside our head, but when the voice appears to come from within, we feel the rules have changed somehow! I don't like being told what to think or feel … even by myself!

Ricardo has a fear of blurting out something in public that could result in catastrophe. He can do in vivo exposure by going to public places and purposely thinking some of his unwanted thoughts. He can do imaginal exposure by writing and reading a script about losing control and saying something that gets him in trouble. But Ricardo has an underlying fear of being *dysregulated* or "off," and this fear comes with a set of compulsions aimed at trying to be certain he is completely in control. He can use interoceptive exposures to practice bringing on the sensations in his body that make him feel uncertain.

Ricardo compulsively breathes slowly and deeply to make himself feel more certain that he'll stay calm. What makes a person feel short of breath? Ricardo can defy his OCD by practicing being short of breath. For example, he could jog in place for a minute before doing his exposures. Another idea—he could breathe through a tiny straw for thirty seconds.

He's also afraid that if his body is too warm, it's a sign that he's about to do something crazy. How can he practice feeling too warm?

_____

He's also afraid that feeling "weird" or dizzy could cause him to accidentally say something damaging. How might he practice putting his body in a state of dizziness or "weirdness"?

_____

more to do

Yay, you helped Ricardo! Another fictional character finally has an effective treatment strategy he can rely on! Okay, now your turn. Take a moment to consider how your OCD makes you *feel*. I don't mean how it makes you feel emotionally (for example, guilty, afraid, embarrassed), but how your body *tells* you that you've been triggered (for example, heaviness in the chest, tension in the shoulders, heat in the face). Remember the basic premise of ERP is trying to create that space between noticing that you're triggered and giving in to your compulsions; we're doing this so we can increase our skills for sitting with uncertainty and *denying* OCD the satisfaction of telling us what to do. In this exercise, we are doing ERP with the body by purposely bringing up the way the body *feels* when it's triggered. Take a moment (and close your eyes if it helps) to remember what it felt like the last time you were triggered by your OCD. See if you can recall what was going on in the body. Use the space below to jot down any ideas you may have for interoceptive exposures that could be useful for you.

_____

_____

_____

_____

_____

_____

_____

_____

Story update: *Interoceptive exposures are ways to generate the uncomfortable feelings that come with OCD so you can get better at having them.*

using brutal, savage, ruthless self-compassion 14

for you to know

All right, so let me get inside that head of yours again. If *mindfulness* is about being able to watch what the mind is doing, observing yourself, then it's sort of like watching yourself as if you were someone else. If you watch someone else suffer and you feel bad, that's called empathy. If you also want that person to suffer less, that's called compassion. So if you're able to watch *yourself,* and you have compassion for others, you are actually capable of having compassion for the *you* that you are watching. *Self*-compassion is exactly this—observing when you are suffering and relating to that suffering the way you might relate to seeing another person suffer. But … it ain't pretty.

I didn't like myself very much as a teenager. I seemed to excel at a lot of things and still feel I wasn't good at anything, and I would constantly chase this feeling of "good enough" wherever I could find it. Mostly this chase manifested in asking a ton of questions and making a ton of jokes about everything. I needed to be seen, but if not everyone liked what they saw (or, worst of all, if *I* didn't like what I saw), I turned on myself. One of the neato things about living with an OCD voice in your head that's constantly criticizing you is that you get really good at criticizing yourself. You learned from the best, your OCD. But the downside is that it can be really hard to shut off once you start. It's like you joined forces with the OCD and then realized this was a mistake, but still, branching off on your own again is terrifying.

One of the reasons we do compulsions is because we fear how harshly we'll treat ourselves later if things don't go our way. This is especially true when obsessions are about moral issues and we imagine doing the "wrong" thing. Saying mean things to yourself when you have an intrusive thought can sometimes feel like the only way to prove you're a good person. *Well, at least I hate myself for being this way, so I can't be all bad...?* So being unkind to yourself is almost always a compulsion, a way to even the score when OCD makes you feel off. Being cool with yourself is therefore the most badass of badass exposures.

for you to do

Being cool with yourself sounds lovely, but how do we actually pull this off? How can we take this instinct to beat up on ourselves and turn it around? One strategy that can help is to catch ourselves in the act (in other words, be mindful of how we're talking to ourselves) and play with language so that it redirects the mind away from self-criticism and into a self-compassionate statement. Think of it like grabbing the wheel from a driver who's passed out and guiding the car back into a lane. Think of the last time you criticized yourself or teamed up with your OCD to make yourself feel bad.

What were you literally thinking about and literally feeling in the moment before you chose to criticize yourself? For example, *I'm thinking I said the wrong thing to my friend and hurt them and am feeling guilty and embarrassed.* Or *I'm thinking I accidentally touched something poisonous and I'm thinking I was stupid and careless.* Notice how you're not actually calling yourself names here, just acknowledging that you are having thoughts about it. Use the space below to write down what you were experiencing in your mind.

_____

Do you think other people feel these things when faced with a challenging situation? I know I feel like a total noob whenever I think I've messed up somehow. See if you can finish this sentence:

Many people in situations like these have thoughts about _____

and feel _____.

What are you not royally screwing up right now? (For example, *I'm doing a pretty good job of resisting compulsions so far even though it's really hard.*)

_____

You can download the template from this activity at http://www.newharbinger .com/46363 to practice self-compassion scripts for multiple situations.

more to do

You can use the exercise above to reorganize unhelpful self-critical and self-punishing thoughts whether they're coming from OCD or not. Just ask yourself to be totally honest about (1) what thoughts and feelings you're actually observing, (2) the fact that other people often think and feel these things when put in similar situations, and (3) that there's something you're doing right even when you're struggling, even if that *something* is just asking for help.

Another useful way to hack into the self-compassion circuits in your brain is to imagine someone you really care about. Maybe it's your best friend or a close relative. Try to picture them dealing with whatever OCD junk your OCD is having you deal with right now. You might not know what advice to give them if you don't know right now how to navigate your OCD, but how would you want them to *think and feel* about themselves if they were in your shoes? Imagine they came to you and told you that they were having this problem you're having right now and they hated themselves for it, thought they were disgusting, evil, stupid, unlovable. Would you say, "Hey, you're spot-on. Keep it up, loser!"? Or, guided by the three earlier points to be honest with yourself about, would you say something more like this: (1) That sounds really hard, (2) I know what that feels like and lots of people get freaked out by stuff like this, and (3) I'm really impressed by how you're coping with this right now.

If you want to put this to the test, pay attention the next time someone shares with you that they're unhappy about something. See what happens when you offer them compassion. Really consider how they respond. If it works for others, it's worth trying on yourself.

Story update: *Being kind to yourself is actually a super effective exposure.*

15 being awesome at not knowing

for you to know

So here we are again in the little box under the title "for you to know." As far back as you or I can remember, we've been taught to collect knowledge in some way. Collecting knowledge, even as babies, is how we make sense of the world. Parents teach us to "know" how to walk, talk, dress ourselves, and so on. Teachers teach us to "know" math, science, writing, and more. And what happens when we acknowledge that we *don't* know something? Someone tells us to find out so we can know it! It's not bad advice, but I wonder, how come nobody ever invites us *not* to know something? Isn't being able to *not know* something and be happy and functional anyway a skill in and of itself? Isn't that the source of joy in watching a magic trick, for example? When you have OCD, *not* knowing (aka being uncertain about) something can feel unbearable. OCD designs it this way to con you into doing compulsions. It's like it, well, *knows* you can't tolerate uncertainty! But it's wrong. You're actually better at dealing with uncertainty than you might think, and enhancing this skill can be your greatest asset in overcoming OCD.

The pilot of an airplane needs to know what all the switches, dials, and buttons do, clearly. But the pilot also needs to be able to handle *not knowing* whether an engine might malfunction or a weather event might suddenly cause turbulence. Being able to sit confidently in the cockpit and *not know* whether something is going to go wrong is what allows the pilot to focus on actually flying the plane. If they are totally consumed by the distress of uncertainty up there, their performance will suffer. The same is true for you. In terms of operating this thing called life, your intolerance, distrust, disgust, and fear of uncertainty is a major distraction from a smooth flight through adolescence.

for you to do

Often it may seem like accepting uncertainty is impossible, unreasonable, or immoral. Trying to be all right with the idea that your worst fear *could* be true is a tall order. But accepting that *something* is possible is only terrifying when we forget that *everything* is possible. In other words, uncertainty is everywhere and embracing this is the key to mastering OCD. Here are some key points to remember about accepting uncertainty:

- **It's not about either/or.** If you can admit that there's a one-in-a-trillion chance that your fear is true, then you are accepting uncertainty. If I told you that there was the same chance that you would win the lottery, you wouldn't rush out to buy tickets. This doesn't mean you wouldn't win. In other words, accepting uncertainty is not a comment on the likelihood of your fears coming true, just a way of acknowledging that you don't have to figure it all out just because OCD tells you to.

- **An exception is an obsession.** If you think you've found an exception to the rule that uncertainty is everywhere, you've found something for your OCD to attach to, that's all. Obsessions aren't special. Obsessions are just ideas you're not comfortable being uncertain about.

- **You accept uncertainty all the time and don't give yourself enough credit.** Almost every moment you're awake, you're dealing with uncertainty really, really gracefully—so much so you don't even notice. Unless your obsession is about *this*, do you really try to know 100 percent what's in your food? Do you really know what toothpaste is made out of? Do you have any idea whether a bird is going to poop on you or a ceiling tile is going to fall on you? I saw my kids get on the bus this morning, but as I sit here in my office writing this, I am only almost-sure they're at school. But if I'm not willing to shrug *that* uncomfortable idea off, I can't be here to write this book now.

- **Confidence is being a badass at uncertainty tolerance.** Any time you enter a situation with your head held high, your shoulders back, and your attitude set to success, you are flexing your uncertainty-tolerating muscles. You are *behaving*

79

like a person who doesn't need to check to make sure that things will go your way. Most of the time when we say we want certainty about something, we really mean we want to *feel confident* about that thing. I feel confident behind the wheel of a car, but this has nothing to do with me being *certain* my left front wheel won't spontaneously explode and yank me into oncoming traffic.

Use the space below to write down things you accept uncertainty about that don't bother you, even though the consequences of being wrong might be really bad. I don't know whether you like this book. I hope you do, but I'm going to accept that you may not, that you may give me a brutal online review, and maybe word will get out that this book is the worst OCD book out there and I'm the worst OCD author. Maybe I'll get "canceled" and nobody will read anything I write ever again because of that "zero stars" you gave me. I'll just go ahead and finish writing it anyway.

_____

_____

_____

_____

_____

_____

_____

more to do

You can make an exposure-based game out of not-knowing. This exercise might be extra difficult if your OCD content is about incompleteness, so it's okay if you want to adjust it to a level that's challenging but tolerable. So the game works like this—pick something that involves taking in information and then choose *not to know* whether you got all of it. For example, flip to a random page of a dictionary and identify a word you've never seen before. Then close the dictionary *before* reading the definition. Or listen to a podcast or an audiobook at twice the speed for a few minutes and don't go back to relisten to words you might have missed. Or watch a few scenes of a foreign language film without subtitles. The purpose of the game is to generate a sense of not-knowing. The more intensely you feel like you're missing something, the better you are at playing the game. This exercise may generate some uncomfortable feelings, but try to think of it as a challenge, like eating something super spicy. This feeling of not-knowing is something you want to be familiar with so you can seek it out when doing ERP.

Story update: *Uncertainty acceptance is a superpower.*

sure, right, whatevs: why reassurance makes you less confident

for you to know

In the last activity, we talked about developing your "not-knowing" skills. Often when we can't seem to convince ourselves our fears are untrue, we turn to others to ask for help. Sometimes this means asking a parent or friend to help us prove our fears away, or sometimes it's hours and hours of googling and scouring the internet for the thing you think will shut down the OCD forever. While a reality check can be helpful sometimes, repeatedly being assured (being *re*assured) that your fears are untrue plays into the OCD. Your brain gets confused. It thinks, "If she keeps telling me something I should already know, then maybe there's something more I need to know!" Learning to resist reassurance seeking is a huge part of winning your freedom back from OCD.

Emily just wanted to be sure she was being a good and decent human being. Scrolling through her social media, she frequently encountered trolls spouting racism, misogyny, and bigotry, and she knew in her heart that she was no troll. The problem was, sometimes she didn't feel like she knew. She might catch herself laughing at an online meme and later realize maybe it wasn't very progressive of her to think something like that was funny. She would sometimes hear her friends at school make comments about the kind of music a certain culture listens to, and she couldn't always tell whether they were talking about it like they liked it or like they looked down on it. If they were bad-mouthing another culture, Emily's OCD said it was totally her responsibility to find out and correct them. Otherwise, it was no different from her being culturally insensitive and that was unacceptable. Her friends would get offended when she'd bring it up, accuse her of being arrogant or judgmental herself. *I'm the least judgmental person in the world!* she would think. That's what OCD demanded, and she had to be sure it was right. Any judgment anywhere in the world had to be rooted out and destroyed. Otherwise, she was A BAD PERSON! (Cue ominous music.)

There were a lot of compulsions Emily engaged in to make herself feel certain she was a good person, like spending hours reading social justice–related things online and checking to make sure she agreed with them, and replaying all her social interactions in her head to make sure she hadn't said or heard anything racist. But the hardest and most disruptive compulsion was asking her mother for reassurance. Sometimes this would come in the form of confessing that she thought she had done something wrong and waiting for her mother to tell her she hadn't. Sometimes it came in the form of a question like, "Would you think I was a bad person if I liked …?" or "Do you think I need to tell so-and-so that they were being culturally insensitive?" or "If I don't correct so-and-so for using insensitive language, does that mean I'm condoning it?"

Mom did her best to answer every question and reassure Emily that she was a kind, loving, and decent human being, the way she raised her to be. But sometimes her mom would get frustrated with her because the questions would keep coming. Mom would get especially upset when Emily would argue with her, like, "But I must be a bad person if I let bad things happen that I could do more to stop … right?"

So every day at school Emily was on edge trying to make sure she was being a good person and every day after school, Emily was on edge trying to get her mom to confirm with 100 percent certainty that she had succeeded in being good. But the more her mom tried to impress upon Emily that she didn't need to worry so much about her morality, that she was good, the less confident Emily felt. "How can I be good when I feel so guilty all the time?"

for you to do

In short, reassurance seeking means getting others to present you, or presenting yourself, with information you already sorta kinda know. It's unlikely you will have made it this far in this workbook without at least *sorta kinda* knowing your unwanted thoughts are about as reliably true as an old man's Twitter rant. It's just that these thoughts so often *feel* true even when they look like nonsense. So you look at the content of your thought and it's like, *I don't need to worry about this*, but then your body is acting like the world is collapsing around you and you think, *Do I need to worry about this? Maybe I do!* Then you go to someone who is less impressed by whatever your OCD is saying and they tell you, "You don't need to worry about this. You're fine." Or maybe you go online and look up something about your obsession and find an article that says you're probably fine. And then your body suddenly quiets the alarm. Feels like relief, like most compulsions do. Then your OCD comes back with, "What does 'probably fine' actually mean?" And the whole cycle starts up again.

The problem is super simple. Your brain interprets reassurance as evidence that there is doubt, that you need to be reminded you're okay because you aren't sure you're okay, and this doubt makes the obsessions seem even more important. If you want to feel confident in your assertion that these unwanted thoughts and feelings are just OCD junk to dismiss, you have to stop sending the signal to your brain that you need to be reminded you're okay. Your favorite athlete doesn't need to be told they can make the shot. They just make the shots over and over again.

Use the space below to write out all the ways you try to get reassurance about your obsession. This can include asking people you know for reassurance, but it may also include consulting Dr. Google, confessing thoughts to get people to tell you it's okay (like Emily), or more indirect things like roping people into conversations about your OCD's theme in the hopes that someone will reassure you.

more to do

You may seek reassurance about your obsession from several people, but many OCD sufferers find themselves choosing one person to be the ultimate reassurance giver. It might be your best friend, the person you're romantically involved with, or a parent. If that person says it's okay, it feels okay for a bit (until it doesn't). Knowing they're in on the scheme to master your OCD can make a huge difference. I'll talk more toward the end of the book about how to talk about your OCD and educate the people around you, but for this activity, let's try to get the message across to this supreme reassurance giver that they can help you resist reassurance moving forward. Your OCD has trapped you and your reassurance giver into a contract that basically says you have to get certain and they have to help you. Use the template below to create a *new* contract that brings you and the reassurance giver into an alliance against the OCD; you can download a copy at http://www.newharbinger.com/46363. On the blank lines, list some alternative statements that would help you resist reassurance seeking, such as "That sounds like one of those questions you wanted me not to answer"; "You're fighting your OCD really hard, I'm proud of you"; "Nice try, OCD, but you're not getting an answer out of me!"; or "I know it's really hard to stand up to OCD, but I believe you can do this." Be as creative as you want here. You know this person best!

Dear _____,

As you know, I ask you a lot of questions about _____ and
expect you to tell me that _____. This makes me feel okay for
a bit, but it turns out it actually makes my unwanted thoughts more powerful in the
end. I am trying really hard to get better at accepting uncertainty about my fears, and
I need your help. Instead of giving me reassurance when I ask about my fears, I want
you to do this:

_____

_____

_____

_____

_____

_____

_____

I give you permission to decide for yourself when I'm asking for reassurance because I
can't always tell for sure. I may not like it when you deny me reassurance, but I know
this is what I need to get better, and I really appreciate your help.

Story update: *Reassurance may look like it helps, but it actually keeps you from overcoming your obsessions.*

17 dear parents, if I have to do ERP, then we all do!

for you to know

One of the great privileges of being a teen is the ability to drive your parents up the wall. Yes, it's sad and painful when it's your OCD that flusters them, but man, it's pretty cool when it's just you being *you*. In my clinical experience, nothing seems to bewilder the parents of a teen client more than when that teen dramatically changes course away from OCD … just because I said so. Imagine your parents' dismay when, after ages of trying to get you to stop doing compulsions and trying to get you to stop worrying so much, you suddenly sprout mindfulness right after reading my book! Okay, okay, I know that's not realistic. It would be fun to see them shaking their heads in confusion when you spontaneously overcome your OCD, but probably we're going to need their help. After all, if you change, they have to change too. Otherwise, *their* old and familiar behaviors could lead you to get stuck in old patterns again.

Alyssa had all the right ingredients for success with her OCD. She recognized that her unwanted thoughts were not her fault and not some indicator of her character or what the future would bring. She educated herself about OCD and even started doing ERP with an OCD therapist. In her sessions with the therapist, she pushed herself to do exposures that were challenging and really worked on letting herself feel the anxiety and embrace the uncertainty. It was super hard, but it helped that she trusted her therapist and knew she wouldn't pressure her to do something unsafe or immoral.

Her therapist would do exposures with her in her office and then she gave Alyssa homework to practice them between sessions, but that was way harder. She had to willingly *choose* to do exposures without anyone nudging or guiding her. She did her best to self-motivate and was able to get into it sometimes, but the anxiety about doing it wrong or going too far would get the best of her. In the therapy office, she knew she wouldn't get to wash or seek reassurance or do other compulsions, but at home, she knew her parents would probably feel so bad about her feeling bad that they would do anything to make her feel better. They couldn't stand to see her in distress, so whenever she felt too triggered, her OCD would say, "Oh, just ask them to reassure you and get it over with." She knew they would. Making matters worse, it was actually triggering for her to know that her anxiety made her parents anxious too. So sometimes she did compulsions just to reassure *them* that she wasn't going to lose it. [Sigh.] If she really expected the hard work of ERP to pay off, she was going to have to train her parents to withstand their *own* discomfort too.

for you to do

There are many ways parents can accommodate OCD symptoms. It's not their fault. They're probably used to accommodating you in lots of ways. *Accommodating* really just means making space for something. Even as I write this at home, there's a kids' movie playing in the background that my daughter appears to be into. I'm accommodating my attention needs so she can enjoy herself and mostly I can just let it gooooo, let it *gooooooo* … Anyway, it's fine. But when parents accommodate compulsions, they're making the *OCD* more comfortable and making it harder for *you* to face it head-on. In Activity 16, we looked at reassurance seeking and how it makes the OCD more confident. Offering you reassurance about your obsession is one way your parents may accommodate your OCD, but there may be many other ways. Here are some common examples of accommodation:

- Buying/replacing items (like soap) when your OCD had you using them excessively

- Helping you avoid triggers (like quickly changing the channel for you if something triggering comes on the TV, or hiding triggering objects so you don't see them)

- Avoiding touching things or talking about things that might be triggering (essentially, following your OCD rules around you)

- Having long, deep conversations with you about your obsession, participating in compulsive analysis of the meaning of your thoughts

- Waiting long periods of time for you to complete a ritual

- Doing chores for you that you could do except your OCD makes it hard

- Checking (for example, lights, locks, appliances) for you

These are just a few ideas. What are some ways your parents may be accommodating your OCD symptoms?

more to do

Learning to watch each other squirm is what makes a family impacted by OCD thrive. If your parents bail you out of OCD situations, they don't do it only to make you feel better. They also do it to ease their own anxiety over knowing their kid is struggling. So if they reduce and ultimately stop giving in to *your* OCD, they have to deal with their *own* fears of not doing enough to ease your pain. So even if they don't have OCD, they still get stuck in a sort of O-C cycle where the obsession is "She needs us and we're not there for her!" and the compulsion is "Here, let me do this for you." In order for your journey to really be a success, you need to be living in an environment made for success. That means everyone needs to break free of their own O-C cycle. Taking some ideas from the list you wrote above, use the form below to start a conversation with your parents about how to reduce accommodations so everyone can get their freedom back from OCD. You'll find a copy you can download at http://www .newharbinger.com/46363.

Hey, I'm ready to really start fighting OCD head-on, and I need your help. In the past, you've done your best to make it easier for me by helping me. (Write ways they accommodate your OCD here.)

_____

_____

_____

Unfortunately, that help is keeping me from retraining my brain to handle my obsessions on its own. It's scary for me to ask you to stop helping, and it's probably scary for you too because it will mean I'll be pretty stressed out sometimes without the help. (Add some kind of thank-you comment for their efforts so far. Parents like that sort of thing.)

_____

_____

_____

So ... I'd like to come up with a plan to gradually reduce the way you accommodate my OCD so I can get stronger. Maybe we can start by:

_____

_____

and then work our way up to:

_____

_____

Like other exposures, it's a great idea to start small. We don't want your parents to be overwhelmed. So, for example, if they're used to doing a chore for you that your OCD says is triggering, you could start reducing the accommodation by doing only a small part of the chore yourself and gradually taking over the job when it feels more manageable for all of you to do so. Using the type of conversation above, keep collaborating with them along the way to always be moving toward freedom from OCD—for all of you.

Story update: *Working to reduce accommodation from your parents is a smart team approach to overcoming OCD.*

why care about self-care 18

for you to know

OCD asks a lot of you. Your parents, teachers, friends, and others all ask a lot of you. So, if it's all right with you, I'd like to just jump in here with my little workbook and … ask a lot of you. If I could go back in time, to the land of Saturday morning cartoons, arcades, and old-fashioned techno, I'd tell myself what I'm about to tell you. Invest in something called the internet. Also, never forget that *you are worth the effort*.

Self-care does not sound cool. It sounds like one of those boring things you're supposed to do that has no immediate payoff, like flossing (you really should floss, by the way). On airplane flights, a standard announcement tells you, in case of an in-flight emergency, to put on your own air mask before helping your kid put on theirs. If you're anything like me, you probably turned your music back on after they said "in-flight emergency" and missed the part about the air masks. The point of the announcement is that you won't do a good job helping anyone else if you're choking to death on toxic fumes as the plane dives into shark-infested waters. The point *I'm* trying to make is that the journey ahead is bumpy, scary, and full of challenges. But we need you. I'm speaking for the planet, humanity, the world economy, and the rest of it. *We all need you*. And if you don't put as much effort into taking care of yourself as you do in caring for us (old people), you won't be *able* to care for us as much as we need you to. That's right, I'm here to encourage you to take care of *yourself* because that's what's in my best interest.

for you to do

Self-care means different things to different people, so not everything in this activity will necessarily apply to you. I've come up with these eight "-ates" here because it's catchy and self-help publishers like stuff like this, but feel free to add anything that makes sense for you personally. The purpose of this activity is to make your self-care options accessible and practical. Take a look at the ideas below and consider how they may apply to you.

- *Activate*—Exercise. Run, cycle, lift, dance, crunch, squat, pull up, push down, do whatever makes you feel strong. Exercise does a lot more than burn calories. It reminds the body that you can have all the same experiences you have when you're anxious (for example, tension, increased heart rate, sweatiness, rapid breathing), but experience them on your own terms—even enjoy them! Exercise can also boost your mood and reduce anxiety. It's great to have a routine, but be mindful not to let OCD turn it into something it's not. It's not about getting the perfect body; doing the exact right number of exercises; or forcing yourself to work out when you're sick, tired, or have other things of value you promised to do.

- *Meditate*—You're probably thinking, *Yeah, he's here again with the meditation.* Seriously, I missed out. I didn't really discover meditation until my thirties, and by then I had so many hardwired mental habits that I'm still working on them today. Meditation changed my life, OCD being only one part of that equation. Learn to meditate now, and you can set the stage for a mind that can really tell the difference between a thought and a threat and really knows how to settle and rest. Long-term benefits aside, taking a little time to meditate, or even just practice mindful games and mindful moments, can improve your mental hygiene and make the present moment less of a burden and more of a gift, even with your OCD around.

- *Medicate*—I'm not here to tell anyone to take or not take any particular medication. Many people with OCD never take psychiatric medication, and many people with OCD do and find that it helps. You can sort that out by talking to a psychiatrist, a medical professional who is an expert in mental health. If you do take medication, take it as prescribed. If it's prescribed to take one a day, take one a day, every day it's prescribed. Most medications that can help with OCD work by maintaining a stable level in your body, so skipping a few days here and there can really interfere in the meds being effective. Whether or not you take medication for OCD, be mindful of any unhealthy *self-medication* strategies you might fall into. Think about what you're putting into your body and whether it is helping you get closer to or further away from the person you want to be.

- *Curate*—Put together an environment that lends itself to pleasurable activities. It may sound pretty basic, but doing things you like that make you feel good and aren't harmful can lead to enjoying things and feeling good! OCD gets the advantage when it corners you into negativity and powerlessness. Boosting your point of view to a sunnier one gives you the advantage over OCD. It turns exposures into *challenges* or opportunities. Some examples: get some sunlight every day, find a way to connect with nature, surround yourself with great music (I like to make playlists for different moods), watch shows and movies that inspire you (I like movies about people's bodies mutating, but maybe you're into rom-coms and that's cool too!), put up artwork or pictures that remind you it's okay to be you … You're actually pretty interesting.

- *Initiate*—Reach out to others and build a social network (a real one with real people you actually know IRL). It doesn't have to be big, and you don't have to be an extrovert to make this happen. This is not a numbers game. Part of self-care is getting out of your echo chamber, letting other people hear and see you, and letting them reflect back to you that you're going to be okay and you're not alone. OCD weaponizes the feeling of solitude to trick you into being its servant. That's pretty metal, I suppose. But my point is, you don't have to suffer alone. Let other people know you.

- *Create*—A great way to make you feel like a god or goddess is to bring things into the world that would never have existed but for you. Make art, make music, write stories, build sculptures, sew, bake, invent—the list goes on. Yes, OCD can make each of these things difficult, especially if you lean toward perfectionism. But then doing all these things also functions as an exposure challenge! Taking care of yourself can mean building a portfolio of sorts. I don't mean for professional reasons, but for internal ones. Knowing you made, are making, or are formulating the idea for making something sends the message to your brain that there are more interesting things to attend to than your OCD. That being said, turning your OCD into something creative steals its thunder too! Sean, the guy who illustrated this book, knows what I'm talking about!

- *Delegate*—Let others take care of their stuff, and some of your stuff too. You don't have to do it all. I'm not talking about avoiding things or having your family members accommodate your OCD. OCD may make you feel like you have to say yes to everything anyone wants from you or suffer the guilt and shame of being a so-called bad or selfish person. But again, how are you supposed to find the energy to put good into the world if you don't take care of yourself? If you are taking on too many responsibilities or doing too many favors, think about how you can ask for help and delegate some stuff to others.

- *Relate*—One of the more interesting ways to take care of yourself is to express kindness to others. Going out of your way to make another person feel better helps build up an instinct toward compassion that works in both directions. Relating to others, or making them feel less alone, can actually make you more inclined to be kind to yourself. The more compassion you develop for yourself, the less capable OCD is of bullying you into compulsions and self-doubt. The more free you get from the OCD, the more compassion you can offer to others. The more they get, the more you get, and so on.

Eight "-ate" words and I didn't even say *graduate*! Not bad! ... But, um, stay in school anyway.

more to do

Not every idea above will necessarily resonate with you. Plus, I only did eight because it rhymes with -ate. Use the space below (or download a copy at http://www .newharbinger.com/46363) to take the ideas above that you liked, plus any other cool ideas you may have for taking good care of yourself, and write a daily self-care cheat sheet that you can keep close by when you need a reminder.

What are things I can do today to stay on top of my self-care game?

_____

_____

_____

_____

_____

_____

_____

_____

_____

Story update: *Paying attention to self-care is an important part of taking the power away from OCD.*

fighting the stigma inside and out 19

for you to know

The therapist who saw me at my worst, and guided me on this path so many years ago, once told me, "OCD's been good to you." I was offended for a brief moment before I realized how much of what I love in my life is an extension of having OCD and having developed some mastery over it. I get to help other people with OCD, give presentations on overcoming OCD, and write books like these. Don't get me wrong—I'm not saying having OCD is some kind of lucky break. But learning to take the lessons of the journey to overcome OCD and apply them to a joyful life is, well, pretty cool.

Most of the adults I've treated first experienced OCD symptoms as a child or teen. Many of those adults didn't find the courage to ask for help for years after the symptoms started. They either didn't know where to look for help because they didn't know they had OCD, or they thought asking for help would be like labeling themselves "defective" for life. That's called stigma, the false, messed-up beliefs people have about mental health.

One thing I've noticed more and more of is teens taking ownership of their OCD and getting involved in advocacy. What could be an endless source of shame and isolation can be turned into a compassion project, a way to ease the suffering of others while continuing to develop your OCD-fighting skills. This can come in many forms. I see teens speaking on stage at venues like the International OCD Foundation's annual conference. Or posting inspirational messages on social media, sharing useful articles, or even running their own online groups. This may not be your thing, and that's totally fine, but one way to fight the stigma inside and out is to be outspoken in your support for others struggling with OCD.

for you to do

As I mentioned above, you're under no pressure whatsoever to be outspoken about OCD or volunteer to be the poster child for it. But if you think it might help you to know you're somehow making it easier for others, consider some ways you can be an advocate or a leader in the OCD community. Can you connect with one other person who has OCD and let them know it's going to be okay? Can you volunteer at an OCD awareness event? Maybe you can start a blog about your treatment journey or contribute to an online support group. True story: I decided to become a therapist because of how much I got out of contributing to an online support group while I was learning to overcome my OCD.

Use the space below to write some ideas of how you can fight mental health stigma.

_____

_____

_____

_____

more to do

Self-stigma is the pits. It's bad enough when society at large has the wrong idea about mental health, but when we do it to ourselves, it's just dreadful. If you take only one lesson away from this book, I hope it's that having OCD doesn't make you crazy, doesn't make you weak, and definitely doesn't make you less-than. It's hard, though, because so many messages about mental health and mental *illness* get thrown around in the media and elsewhere, you can't help but absorb some of it. So you start relating to having any "mental health condition" like it's so much worse than some physical condition, which is especially weird because OCD is so common and treatable! If you're thinking it's okay for *other* people to have mental health challenges, but it's not okay for *you*, you may be promoting the very thing that keeps others from getting help. Think of all the times you needed support but didn't allow yourself to reach out because you didn't want people to know, or assumed they'd judge you. And what about all the times you chose to give in to compulsions just because you were afraid of how badly you'd treat *yourself* if your distress level became noticeable to others?

What are some ways you may stigmatize yourself?

_____

_____

What could you do differently to fight that self-stigma?

_____

_____

Story update: *A world with less stigma around mental health is a world where you treat yourself better too.*

one activity to rule them all: your basic plan for tackling any obsession 20

for you to know

One of OCD's nastier tricks is to make your obsession seem like it isn't OCD. Even if you see a chapter in an OCD workbook that comes super close to describing your OCD theme, it may seem like yours is just a *little* bit different. Too different for your OCD! The thing is, once you understand the core concepts laid out in the previous activities, you can design your own treatment plan for *any* OCD content. Check this out.

for you to do

Behold—the most workbooky part of the workbook awaits you in the pages ahead! Let's do a quick review of the core concepts you need to know to stand up to OCD, and then you can input the details of whatever obsession arises whenever you are ready to tackle it.

You can go back to any activity earlier in this book and get a deeper understanding of the OCD-fighting concepts you need to know. Here I've distilled the bulk of the ideas into five concepts. Read them over and ask yourself whether this approach makes sense. If it doesn't, that's all good; just go back to an earlier activity where it is explained in more detail.

Concept 1: My diagnosis, or *O to the C to the D.*

Obsessions are unwanted thoughts, feelings, and sensations. *Compulsions* are ways you try to be certain about them. Obsessions feed off compulsions, which leads to stronger obsessions and stronger urges to do compulsions … creating a loop called the obsessive-compulsive cycle. *Disorder* is the word we use to describe this loop getting in our way. You can review Activities 1–6 to lock down this concept.

Concept 2: Mindfulness, or *Hey, look at that, a thought!*

Thoughts, feelings, and sensations in the body are all just experiences you "see" in the mind. Mindfulness is the skill of viewing your obsessions and your urges to do compulsions simply as experiences to be observed, not threats, warnings, or judgments. If you practice mindful exercises (such as meditation), you can strengthen this skill. You can review Activities 7 and 8 to lock down this concept.

Concept 3: Thinking about your experiences, or *If you are aware of the way you think, you can change the way you think about what you think!*

If you are paying attention to what's coming up in the mind, you are being mindful. If you are being mindful, you may notice thinking patterns that make you more likely to give in to compulsions. These unhelpful patterns are called cognitive distortions and challenging them can help you remain mindful and make less compulsive choices. You can review Activities 9 and 10 to lock down this concept.

Concept 4: Self-compassion and self-care, or *I like you, so you should like you too.*

You don't choose which thoughts, feelings, and sensations to have. Being hard on yourself means being confused about your role in having thoughts, feelings, and sensations. Being self-compassionate means being clear about this and treating yourself like you would treat someone you care about. You can review Activities 14, 18, and 19 to lock down this concept.

Concept 5: ERP, or *You can beat any obsession by strengthening your not-knowing skills.*

An obsession is just an idea that you feel uncapable or unwilling to be uncertain about. Getting better at being uncertain is how you overcome an obsession. Getting to the core of what it is you're uncertain about and practicing being uncertain about it is called exposure. Resisting compulsions while you do this is called response prevention. Exposure and response prevention (ERP) is how you teach the brain to react differently to your triggers. You can review Activities 11–13 and 15–17 to lock down this concept.

more to do

Armed with a basic grasp of these concepts, let's take your obsession and plug it into your own personalized self-treatment plan. You can download this worksheet at http://www.newharbinger.com/46363.

Step 1: What exactly is my OCD's deal?

I have a fear of/have intrusive thoughts of/don't like uncertainty about:

_____

_____

To escape my fear/avoid thinking about/get more certain about this, I:

_____

_____

Compulsions keep my obsessions alive, so I am going to stand up to my OCD and execute a plan that catches and stops my compulsions.

Step 2: How can I boost my mindfulness skills to prepare for mastery over my OCD?

It's easier to resist compulsions when I remember that thoughts are just thoughts, feelings are just feelings, and sensations are just sensations. I can practice viewing things this way with meditation and meditation games like:

_____

_____

_____

_____

_____

Today I am willing to commit this amount of time to mindfulness practice.

_____

Sticking to the present moment instead of being lost in thought is a super-skill. *I get to choose what to do with my attention, not OCD!*

Step 3: How can I challenge the thinking that leads to compulsions?

Here are things I sometimes think when I'm triggered:

_____

_____

_____

Here are styles of thinking (cognitive distortions) that tend to get in my way:

_____

_____

_____

Here's a way to think about it that helps me accept uncertainty and resist compulsions (without being too reassuring!):

_____

_____

_____

I can challenge my OCD assumptions and choose a noncompulsive path even though it's scary. Here are some ways I can respond to unwanted thoughts without going on the defensive:

_____

_____

_____

_____

Step 4: How can I use compassion to empower myself?

I didn't choose this fight, but I'm going to win it. Being self-compassionate removes the distraction of self-hatred, and that's all self-hatred is, a distraction! Many people struggle with obsessions and compulsions. I'm already doing something great by reading this book and plotting my next steps. Here are some other things I'm already doing a pretty kickass job of:

_____

_____

_____

_____

_____

_____

Here are some things I actually like about myself that might be assets in the battles ahead:

_____

_____

_____

Step 5: How will I use ERP for world domination?

Ah yes, big scary ERP! Aka kicking the OCD where it counts! I don't choose my thoughts, feelings, or sensations, and it's not my fault that I am conditioned to have this challenge, but I *can* choose to change this conditioning with ERP. (Now would be a great time to check out the in vivo, imaginal, and interoceptive exposure activities again.)

I can practice in vivo exposures by:

_____

_____

_____

_____

_____

_____

And today I can start with something manageable like:

_____

_____

_____

I can write a script about:

_____

_____

_____

And today I can read it this many times while resisting compulsions:

_____

I can generate the icky feelings my OCD uses to bully me with by:

_____

_____

_____

I can get my parents on board with reducing accommodations like:

_____

_____

_____

Need some ideas? Below are some ERP strategies for a few common OCD themes. These are just a few strategies, of course, and you can think of more. Also, every one of these categories can include collaborating with your parents on cutting out the reassurance seeking and accommodating of compulsions.

Contamination obsessions—Having a fear of or big disgust reaction to some of the things we encounter in this world is super common. Things get out of hand when we try to be *certain* we're clean, safe, or responsible. Whether it's germs, chemicals, bodily fluids, or something else your OCD makes difficult to deal with, exposures that help you practice feeling contaminated are the key to getting better!

- Touching triggering items and resisting washing

- Touching triggering items and then touching a bunch of "clean" items

- Placing triggering items where they are likely to be touched

- Skipping or changing your washing/cleaning rituals to break OCD rules

Sexual obsessions—Unwanted and upsetting thoughts/feelings/sensations around being attracted to things that don't make sense can be terrifying! But it's really common in the OCD world. Could be thoughts about something that doesn't align with your sexual orientation, or thoughts about little kids, animals, you name it—if your OCD likes to taunt you with this content, taunt it back with ERP!

- Staying away from googling and other forms of reassurance seeking about your obsession

- Listening to music or watching shows that trigger the thoughts

- Writing imaginal scripts about the sexual obsessions being real

- Agreeing with thoughts as they arise or shrugging them off instead of trying to figure them out

Violent thoughts—Holy crap, these can blindside you if you don't already know you have OCD! Or even if you already knew you had OCD! Unwanted, intrusive thoughts about stabbing, shooting, poisoning, or otherwise harming people (including yourself, aww man, that's just, ugh) can all be overcome by outwitting your OCD with ERP.

- Cutting out avoidance of triggering objects

- Watching movies with triggering violent scenes

- Writing scripts about your fears coming true (or secretly wanting them to!)

- Catching and abandoning reassurance seeking and mental rituals used to figure out whether or not you did/would/can/could/might/may harm anyone!

Religious/moral scrupulosity—Not everyone has religious obsessions, but pretty much every person I've ever met with OCD gets stuck on the tiny details of life's "rules" or guidelines. If it's religious rules, you may struggle with intrusive thoughts about who or what you worship, or you may worry excessively that you're committing sins. If it's morality rules you get stuck on, you may worry about being perfectly honest, or keep dwelling on whether you did the perfect moral thing. OCD would love for you to burn through your adolescence feeling bad all the time for no reason. I think a better idea would be to make the OCD feel bad with ERP!

- Writing scripts about rules you may be breaking

- Eliminating checking and reassurance compulsions to make sure you're following the rules

- Breaking/bending rules that are meant to be more flexible than your OCD says (You may need some initial advice on this from someone who understands the rules you're working with.)

- Making triggering thoughts worse or funny when they come up

Relationship-themed obsessions—So dating is a thing, apparently. From what I see in pretty much every movie and show or hear in pretty much every song, we're expected to pair up somehow. But OCD sometimes likes to bully you with thoughts about being in the wrong relationship, choosing the wrong person, or liking someone too much or not enough. OCD is a pretty awful and annoying tagalong on a date!

- Writing scripts about being in the wrong relationship

- Agreeing with unwanted thoughts about the relationship (but behaving the opposite way!)

- Resisting reassurance seeking about the quality of the relationship

- Reducing (or increasing—whatever's scarier!) texts or other contact with your partner

Just-right and sensorimotor obsessions—Sometimes the OCD doesn't come at you with a clear-cut fear but more of just a general sense that if you don't do a compulsion, you'll be uncomfortable or unhappy with no end in sight. These can come in the form of feeling like you have to do everything in a certain order or number of times, or repeat things until they feel "complete" to you. Or sometimes, as in sensorimotor obsessions, it can feel like you just can't stop paying attention to your blinking or breathing or some other sensation in the body. It may seem weird to you, but it's just another way OCD can show up. Instead of trying to get things right, you can use ERP to get better at leaving things weird!

- Practicing doing things in the "wrong" way, number, or order—getting better at feeling incomplete or off

- Agreeing with unwanted thoughts about always thinking about your triggers, always feeling off or different

- Setting up randomized reminders to trigger you into remembering what's triggering you

- Scripting about the consequences of never resolving your obsessions

Obviously, the types of obsessions we can have are limited only by our imagination, and you have a big imagination. I can't give examples for every possible brand of OCD here. If yours wasn't included in the samples above, that doesn't make it weird. It just makes *me* lazy. Take *your* OCD content and plug it in to this activity. You're better at this OCD-fighting stuff than you think!

Story update: *Any kind of OCD can be overcome if you bring the right tools together!*

One More Thing ...

So, listen. I know you didn't go through this workbook and come out the other side free from OCD. But I hope you learned some things about yourself and picked up some tools for standing up to the disorder. I want to leave you with some advice I wish I had when I was careening into adulthood with OCD. Remember, above all that self-hatred is a fraud perpetrated on you by the OCD. Don't let the philosophical errors that come from a life with OCD become your personality. What do I mean by philosophical errors? I mean how you see yourself, the world, and the relationship between the two. Don't let it make you cynical. The world isn't made of trash just because it has trash in it. Don't let it make you pessimistic. "Nothing ever goes my way" is not a worldview. Don't let it *ever* trick you into thinking that what you're feeling now you'll feel forever. And if you *do* get tricked, don't let that be a reason to hate yourself either. Finally, remember, you are never truly alone. You've never had an unwanted thought that wasn't shared by someone somewhere at some time. And you are never without a path to OCD mastery. Sometimes you just need a guide or a skillfully pointed flashlight. I hope this book shines some light in the direction you need.

Jon Hershfield, MFT, is director of The Center for OCD and Anxiety at Sheppard Pratt in Towson, MD. He specializes in the use of mindfulness and cognitive behavioral therapy (CBT) for obsessive-compulsive disorder (OCD) and related disorders. He is author of *Overcoming Harm OCD*, *When a Family Member Has OCD*, and *The OCD Workbook for Teens*; and coauthor of *The Mindfulness Workbook for OCD* and *Everyday Mindfulness for OCD*.

Illustrator **Sean Shinnock** is a freelance artist/illustrator, advocate, and project developer currently living in Boston, MA.

FROM OUR PUBLISHER—

As the publisher at New Harbinger and a clinical psychologist since 1978, I know that emotional problems are best helped with evidence-based therapies. These are the treatments derived from scientific research (randomized controlled trials) that show what works. Whether these treatments are delivered by trained clinicians or found in a self-help book, they are designed to provide you with proven strategies to overcome your problem.

Therapies that aren't evidence-based—whether offered by clinicians or in books—are much less likely to help. In fact, therapies that aren't guided by science may not help you at all. That's why this New Harbinger book is based on scientific evidence that the treatment can relieve emotional pain.

This is important: if this book isn't enough, and you need the help of a skilled therapist, use the following resources to find a clinician trained in the evidence-based protocols appropriate for your problem. And if you need more support—a community that understands what you're going through and can show you ways to cope—resources for that are provided below, as well.

Real help is available for the problems you have been struggling with. The skills you can learn from evidence-based therapies will change your life.

Matthew McKay, PhD
Publisher, New Harbinger Publications

**If you need a therapist, the following organization
can help you find a therapist trained in cognitive behavioral therapy (CBT).**

The Association for Behavioral & Cognitive Therapies (ABCT) Find-a-Therapist service offers a list of therapists schooled in CBT techniques. Therapists listed are licensed professionals who have met the membership requirements of ABCT and who have chosen to appear in the directory.
Please visit www.abct.org and click on *Find a Therapist*.

**For additional support for patients, family, and friends,
please contact the following:**

International OCD Foundation (IOCDF)
Visit www.ocfoundation.org